Navigating Cultural Competence
in **Grades K–5**

A Compass for Teachers

NANCY P. GALLAVAN

Foreword by Francisco Rios

CORWIN
A SAGE Company

For information:

Corwin
A SAGE Company
2455 Teller Road
Thousand Oaks, California 91320
(800) 233-9936
Fax: (800) 417-2466
www.corwin.com

SAGE India Pvt. Ltd.
B 1/I 1 Mohan Cooperative
  Industrial Area
Mathura Road, New Delhi 110 044
India

SAGE Ltd.
1 Oliver's Yard
55 City Road
London EC1Y 1SP
United Kingdom

SAGE Asia-Pacific Pte. Ltd.
33 Pekin Street #02-01
Far East Square
Singapore 048763

Printed in the United States of America.

Library of Congress Cataloging-in-Publication Data

Gallavan, Nancy P.
Navigating cultural competence in grades K-5: a compass for teachers/Nancy P. Gallavan; foreword by Francisco Rios.
    p. cm.
Includes bibliographical references and index.
ISBN 978-1-4129-7849-1 (pbk.)

    1. Multicultural education—United States. 2. Multiculturalism—Study and teaching (Elementary)—United States. I. Title.

LC1099.3.G355 2011
370.1170973—dc22   2010031219

This book is printed on acid-free paper.

10   11   12   13   14   10   9   8   7   6   5   4   3   2   1

Acquisitions Editor:	Jessica Allan
Associate Editor:	Allison Scott
Production Editor:	Cassandra Margaret Seibel
Copy Editor:	Gretchen Treadwell
Typesetter:	C&M Digitals (P) Ltd.
Proofreader:	Christine Dahlin
Indexer:	Jean Casalegno
Cover Designer:	Scott Van Atta

Contents

Foreword

The most pressing issues in American public education continue to center around how to provide the most meaningful and appropriate education for students and their families, especially those from groups that have been historically and contemporarily marginalized by schools. Among these include students whose families have low-incomes, students for whom English is not a primary language, and students from ethnically and culturally diverse backgrounds.

Teachers are the most important key to providing this meaningful and appropriate education. Teachers can work with their students to develop caring relationships, promote critical thinking skills, assure academic skill development, and engage in the broader community to address pressing social challenges. And the best teachers find ways to do all of these during a school year.

Accomplishing these ends is no simple feat. It is complicated when teachers do not come from nor fully understand the students (as well as their families and the communities) in their charge. It is complicated by the limitations of their own education when it does not effectively prepare them to cross cultural boundaries competently. Even when teachers have developed this competence, it is complicated by the pressing demands placed on teachers: the emphasis placed on limited accountability measures to gauge what students know, the implementation of a scripted curricula which undermines pedagogical creativity, and the press to conform to top-down educational mandates and reforms.

What is needed, now more than ever, is direction to teachers in order to achieve the ideals that they have for themselves and for their students. These ideals need to include helping every student to achieve academic excellence and to realize their full potential. But these ideals also need to include the character and courage required to assure that democracy, equity, and social justice permeate their work (classroom and school-community) environment.

I am honored to provide the foreword to this book, *Navigating Cultural Competence in Grades K–5*. Nancy Gallavan brings to this task a broad understanding of the role educators must play in assuring that the excellence they seek is accompanied by equity and social justice. I appreciate that this work acknowledges the complexity of this work: the challenges associated with responding to continual change, combating persistent forms of oppression, and teaching for equity and justice.

The idea of "navigating" is a productive analogy for the work of teachers. In preparing to teach, you most likely have a map that provides a general lay of the land in education. Only when you arrive at the places (classrooms, schools, and communities) where you find yourself will you see the full details of these milieu: the individuals who inhabit these spaces, the specific challenges and opportunities of being there, and the skills and knowledge that will help you to not only survive but to thrive.

This book also provides a set of skills and knowledge that will help you to navigate the different terrains you will encounter. Teachers today, beyond being experts in teaching, learning, and curriculum, need a variety of other skills to be successful in school settings. *Navigating Cultural Competence in Grades K–5* provides you with an opportunity to develop these skills associated with affirming difference, building community, fostering professionalism, and pursuing social justice.

At end, however, having the skills, knowledge, tools, and desires to pursue a direction can never fully prepare you for the actual journey. Life as a teacher is full of the unexpected, the uncertain, and the unknown. Teachers are, after all, dealing with people (students, colleagues, school staff, administrators, caregivers, community activists, etc.) and institutions (schools) that can never fully be "knowable." Rather than stopping you from the journey, it is better that you embrace the unknown. Strong in purpose and clear in focus, your journey begins with a single step. Forging strong, positive relationships with all those around you assures that you'll never be lost and never feel alone.

The Spanish poet Antonio Machado described this journey aptly:

Caminante, son tus huellas

el camino, y nada más;

caminante, no hay camino,

se hace camino al andar.

Al andar se hace camino,

y al volver la vista atrás

se ve la senda que nunca

se ha de volver a pisar.

Caminante, no hay camino,

sino estelas en la mar.

Wanderer, your footsteps are
the road, and nothing more;
wanderer, there is no road,
the road is made by walking.
By walking one makes the road,
and upon glancing behind
one sees the path
that never will be trod again.
Wanderer, there is no road—
Only wakes upon the sea.

Francisco Rios, Director
Social Justice Research Center
University of Wyoming
August, 2010

Preface

Becoming a teacher has been a lifelong dream for you. Now, whether you are starting your first, fifth, or fifteenth year of teaching, you are focused on becoming the best teacher you can be. You want to be successful and feel satisfaction having achieved efficacy with all students and their families. However, your journey to improving your efficacy is always unfolding ahead of you. The path through your career is accompanied with surprises, challenges, discoveries, and rewards that never cease to amaze you. At this time, you may be concerned primarily about teaching a lesson effectively and efficiently while keeping everyone on task. Yet, simultaneously, you are focused on creating a warm and welcoming sense of place where students experience curiosity and express their own creativity.

Schools and classrooms continue to change. The changes include who is coming to school, what is being taught, how it is being taught, and how learning is both conveyed and assessed. Although you have built upon your past memories of when you started your teaching career, you quickly realized that contemporary schools and classrooms involve new and different complexities for which you have no or limited background or experiences. These sensations happen to all teachers, and this book will help you bridge from your past, fortify you for the present, and prepare you for the future.

To fulfill all of your dreams along your travels as a teacher, you are navigating cultural competence. Cultural competence encompasses teaching and learning about all people, places, things, and events; these experiences are both like and unlike the ones that are known, understood, accepted, and promoted with dignity and respect.

Through cultural competence, teachers provide guidance for achieving proficiency in all endeavors, encouragement for demonstrating proficiencies through individual forms of expression, and assurance for maintaining positive regard for all individuals and groups. In schools and classrooms, cultural competence entails the knowledge, skills, dispositions, and expressions (or what we know, do, believe, and respect) about ourselves, others, and all members of society; these are demonstrated through our thoughts, words, actions, and interactions.

In other words, cultural competence involves the content, practices, and contexts for achieving success and sensing satisfaction for that which is significant, as well as sustaining success and satisfaction throughout one's schooling. You want your students to enjoy school and to learn. Hopefully, you also want to enjoy school and learn along with your students. Navigating cultural competence equips you with the tools to share the journey with your students so all students will be academically accomplished, individually rewarded, and socially accepted during their school years—and throughout their lives.

Historically, schools and classrooms across the United States have not always been safe environments where all students were motivated to attend and achieve. Not all schools and classrooms taught about or practiced (1) democratic principles, (2) educational equity, (3) human rights, and (4) social justice ensuring that each of these goals was granted to each student. Shamefully, some contemporary schools and teachers still continue to be challenged, if not reluctant, and even resistant in fulfilling these goals.

As a classroom teacher, you must fulfill each of these four goals; this text explains the rationale and provides the strategies to achieve efficacy. When you practice cultural competence, your teaching and the learning in your classroom will be successful; everyone—including you—will achieve a sense of satisfaction. You and your students will know what is significant and will be able to sustain individual success and satisfaction.

This text should assure you that you will become one of the best teachers possible. As you read each chapter, reflect upon your past and review the items in the suitcase that you have brought with you. Some of those suitcases are packed with excellent practices; some of those suitcases contain practices that you are encouraged to modify or leave behind.

In your suitcase, you will find three categories of practices with positive and negative influences:

1. The generational perpetuation of practice (Gallavan, 2007): In your journey as a teacher, you may replicate the messages and methods that your own teachers exhibited. Be aware that you may be perpetuating practices that need to be modified or stopped. This trend applies particularly to new teachers who are prepared and then start their careers in the same geographic regions where they were raised. If this pattern applies to you, you are strongly encouraged to read about and preferably visit many other schools and classrooms across the United States.

2. The apprenticeship of observation (Lortie, 1975): Although you learned from your mentors and colleagues, it is time for you to recognize and distinguish the practices that are helpful from the practices that are harmful. Choose carefully; it is easy to follow a leader who is not the best one for you to follow. Teachers tend to establish the foundations of their practices early with little or no change in their careers.

3. The poverty of practice (Black & Wiliam, 1998): Not only must you distinguish the practices that contribute to your efficacy from the practices that detract from your efficacy, you must realize that some desired practices just don't exist in today's schools and classrooms. This is called the poverty of practice. You are encouraged to enroll in graduate courses at a university, travel near and far, and visit schools to talk with teachers who are achieving cultural competence. In addition, you can read books, search the Internet, and form a study group with teachers like yourself. The resources are endless. If you want to improve the strong positive influences generated through the generational perpetuation of practice and apprenticeship of observation, you will need to nourish the poverty of your practice.

AUDIENCE

This book is written for classroom teachers at all stages of their careers. It is particularly useful as a text for a study group, for professional development, or for mentoring new teachers and interns. Cultural competence is not a new idea and most teachers have studied multicultural education in various ways. However, the time has come for all teachers to become culturally competent and commit to ensuring that their students also become culturally competent.

This book equips you with the Gallavan cultural competence compass so you can navigate your career, guaranteeing success and satisfaction for you, your students, their families, and school administrators. You want your students (and yourself) to enjoy your classroom every day. This book will help you follow that dream.

Acknowledgments

The author would like to thank her many colleagues, students, teacher, and young learners who have shared the journey while navigating cultural competence. Only through other people's experiences could the author write this text. Nancy heartily thanks her husband, Richard, for the many intriguing and insightful conversations; and her colleagues Porter, María, Angela, Stephanie, and Wendy for sharing their personal experiences and professional discoveries. Special appreciation is extended to Dr. Edith W. King at the University of Denver for her dedication to cultural competence and support of my research through her worldmindedness.

PUBLISHER'S ACKNOWLEDGMENTS

Corwin gratefully acknowledges the contributions of the following reviewers:

James Becker
Teacher, Administrator
Branksome Hall
Toronto, Ontario
Canada

Diane Senk
ELL/Reading Teacher
Sheboygan Area School District
Sheboygan, WI

About the Author

 **Nancy P. Gallavan** worked as an elementary and middle school teacher in the St. Vrain Valley and Cherry Creek School Districts of Colorado for twenty years while earning her MA from the University of Colorado and her PhD from the University of Denver. Prior to her current position, she was an associate professor of teacher education, specializing in social studies and multicultural education at the University of Nevada, Las Vegas. She has authored more than eighty publications, including books, chapters, and articles in professional education journals, including *Developing Performance-Based Assessments, Grades K–5* (2009); *Developing Performance-Based Assessments, Grades 6–12* (2009); *Secrets to Success for Elementary School Teachers* (2007); and *Secrets to Success for Social Studies Teachers* (2008) with Ellen Kottler, all with Corwin Press. She is active in the American Educational Research Association (AERA), the Association of Teacher Educators (ATE), the National Association for Multicultural Education (NAME), and the National Council for the Social Studies (NCSS), along with regional and state associations. Currently, she is a professor of teacher education in the Master of Arts of Teaching (MAT) program at the University of Central Arkansas.

Introduction

Competence encompasses one's ability to demonstrate proficiency in a particular area and with specific tasks. In this book, the area is culture and the tasks are teaching, learning, and schooling. Just like all other school subjects, teachers need to be fully prepared with the knowledge, skills, and dispositions necessary to achieve efficacy with cultural competence in all contexts. This means a teacher needs to understand and accept one's responsibilities for each student's engagement, expressions, and outcomes across the curriculum, instruction, assessments, and management, as all of these intertwine with culture. Accepting responsibility means striving for efficacy related to teaching and each student's learning.

Culture is a part of everything that is taught and caught. Teachers must be equipped to honor and respect each student's culture; to teach about culture as content and the processes of culturally interacting with one another; to build upon each student's acquisition, application, and appreciation of culture; and to infuse the content, processes, and context of culture across the entire curriculum. In order to accomplish these outcomes, teacher candidates need to be aware of their own understanding, interactions, and attitudes.

This book was written to broaden your knowledge about cultural diversity so you can reach all of your students as you teach them about themselves and one another as young learners. Your background and experiences encase your story; as a classroom teacher, it is essential to increase your awareness of every student's story. This book guides you with the depth to empower each of your students with the information, access, and opportunities each one of them needs and wants to be successful in your classroom and throughout their lives.

The intention is to provide you with information, insights, and inspiration so you are both comfortable with the conversation and confident in your teaching. However, given the history of, conversations about, and conflicts associated with culture in the United States and around the world, delving into cultural competence becomes a lifelong journey more than a completed item on a packing list or a predetermined destination. Thus, the title of the book is *Navigating Cultural Competence*, providing you with tools and techniques as you travel through your teaching career in all areas related to culture.

Be reassured that navigating cultural competence is a learned expertise that must be negotiated with every new encounter and experience. This book was written specifically to guide you as you embark on your career using the Gallavan cultural competence compass. Each of the eight points on the compass identifies one of the essential directions you must consider and coordinate for safe travels.

Just as a compass helps you find your way through the elements of land, water, space, and time, the process of navigating cultural competence involves four critical elements that include:

Concepts. Significant information and initiatives about cultural competence based on theory, research, and practice.

Awareness. Honest inquiries and insights about oneself, one another, and society that occur frequently and easily.

Reflection. Clear evidence and impressions generated by watching, listening, and reading to assess and record process thoroughly.

Education. Meaningful inspirations and influences to ensure that cultural competence is natural, authentic, and holistic.

Looking at the first letters of these four components, you see that they spell the word *CARE*. Navigating cultural competence requires care for yourself, one another, and all of society—near and far, known and unknown. As a teacher, you need to care about your students, your teaching, and their learning in the context of schooling and the world. This book will equip you with many reasons to focus on CARE.

Each chapter in this text features the introduction of new concepts, prompts for expanding awareness, opportunities for reflection, and connections to one's education. To strengthen your care for navigating cultural competence to achieve efficacy, each chapter opens with frequently asked questions with answers, and then closes with extending activities for yourself and learning experience ideas for your young learners. From these resources, you can align your curriculum, instruction, and assessments while building a community of learners and managing your classroom so every day is a rewarding preparation for tomorrow.

Chapters 1 and 2 define cultural competence, debunk ten preconceptions to which teachers tend to ascribe, and introduce the Gallavan cultural competence compass. The best and proper tool to take on any journey is a compass. The eight points of the compass are used as the main points for Chapters 3 through 8. In each chapter, you will find a description of the compass point, key points, and specific strategies; these conclude with frequently asked questions and two groups of activities. One group of activities allows you to expand your own professional understanding and teaching expertise, and one group of activities can enrich your students' understanding and learning experiences.

Chapters 1 and 2 also establish a sense of place to explore cultural competence. This book is based on a set of purposes and goals that you must relate to your own personal, professional, and pedagogical growth and development. Navigating cultural competence necessitates balancing internal perceptions with external stimuli. As a teacher, you provide these opportunities for your students in everything that is taught and caught.

Chapter 3 delves into noticing culture and cultural characteristics. This chapter helps you start your trip by increasing your awareness of the world around you. This is gained through all five of your senses, as well as expanding your thinking, while enhancing your feelings with your emotions. Then, you move into Chapter 4, which explores negotiating and evaluating the curriculum and content. Here, you will extend your understanding of cultural competence to your classroom subject areas as an independent subject area, and an infused highlight to everything you are teaching. Regardless of what you teach and how you are teaching, you will infuse cultural competence across your curriculum, instruction, and assessments.

Chapter 5 captures one of the most important ideas in this text. Here, you will gain insight for establishing a sense of place. Your teaching will be totally ineffective if your students do not attend school or fail to engage in their learning. You want your students to be excited about attending school and motivated about learning and sharing their new discoveries. This chapter reveals the techniques connected with cultural competence so every student achieves success and satisfaction that is sustained throughout your school year.

Chapter 6 offers strategies for seeking and engaging in collaborative endeavors with your colleagues, and for constructing new approaches with your colleagues, with your students, and on your own. Navigating cultural competence means getting involved in the process and working with other teachers to make changes and improve your efficacy both in and out of the classroom. You will be impressed with the amount of time you gain when you meet with your colleagues to share the work, the results, and the rewards. This is a chapter full of new approaches to make your life much easier and more rewarding.

Chapter 7 shares techniques to spark conversations and climate with colleagues and students, and most important, your students' families.

Soon you will discover that you and your students will be more successful when the students' families are involved. Involvement means many different outcomes for different students and families; this chapter explores the possibilities. Once you model to your students and show them the fascination and enjoyment to learn *about* other people and *with* other people, teaching and learning take on a new life of their own. This chapter reveals the encouragement you need and want to make your classroom resonate.

Chapter 7 also prepares you to strengthen and weave together the complexities and controversies that abound in schools and classrooms, particularly those concerns associated with cultural competence. The United States has a history of changes in population demographics, group acceptance, and individual rights. You have likely taken an array of history, political science, sociology courses, and so forth, where you delved into many of the country's issues. Now you will integrate the learning into your classroom. You want the processes to be positive and productive.

Chapter 8 opens doors to help you waken compassion and commitment—both for yourself and with your young learners. Incorporating cultural competence into your classroom is admirable; now you can connect the classroom with communities, near and far. The guidelines provided in the chapter assist you in maintaining your momentum after your initial interest has disappeared. It is vital for you to infuse cultural competence across the curriculum and connect it with your students both in and out of the classroom. Tapping into their compassion to care for other people and society, and fortifying their commitment, will be one of your greatest challenges.

Chapter 8 also provides important guidelines to nurture and welcome challenges and changes. Teaching is dynamic and every day brings new surprises. This chapter prepares you to use challenges and changes to your advantage. Keep in mind that navigating cultural competence is both a journey and a destination; therefore, life will bring you endless challenges and changes that you not only welcome, but you may even instigate. The guidance in this chapter is intended for after you have learned the information in the previous chapters by design. Now the text returns to focusing on you, just as the text began.

At the end of the book, there are three resources. Resource A presents the Gallavan cultural competence compass referenced throughout the text. The cultural compass has been dissected in Chapters 3 through 8 so you can focus on the particular direction points. Resource B provides a review checklist, while Resource C supplies a list of websites related to cultural competence; cultural competence involves a field of study that has existed since time began. Cultural competence is an intricate part of your success in your classroom, professional development, and graduate studies. These readings and references will help you.

My wish is that you will read this text with an open and accepting mind. I hope that you will consider the ideas and try implementing them into your personal life, professional growth, and pedagogical endeavors. Each of us was born with cultural competence. We all wanted and needed dignity, respect, and care. As we grew, we reproduced and returned exactly what we saw and heard. For many of us, cultural competence was not honored or practiced so we have been limited in our lives and our work, perhaps cowering away from doing the right thing. As teachers, we need to ensure that all students are valued and everything that is taught reflects the cultures of all peoples. This book provides the cultural compass to guide you as you navigate your travels.

Kendall is a first grade teacher in her seventh year of teaching. She successfully completed the required multicultural education course during her teacher education program at a nearby university almost ten years ago. In her vague memory, it seems like the course content covered a broad range of topics and issues along with some curricular and instructional practices. However, she learned much more about multicultural education when she got into a classroom.

This week, Kendall has been assigned an intern from the university, named Parker, who shared a list of expectations that includes describing evidence of cultural competence in Kendall's classroom. Parker explained that cultural competence centers on valuing diversity in every student so all students learn about themselves, one another, and society in ways that ensure engagement, excellence, and equity. He added that the criteria of cultural competence state that evidence should be honest, natural, authentic, and holistic.

Kendall started thinking about her classroom in terms of cultural competence, noting that she needs to revisit her purposes and practices. She has always considered herself attentive to providing for her students' academic achievements, but her students' test scores are not improving.

Kendall admits to herself that she does not always take the time to get to know each student as well as she should, although she readily recognizes that students learn more content and demonstrate greater achievement when she and her students are connected. Kendall also confesses that she does not know much about people who are unlike her. Kendall is a White, European American, middle-class, married woman with one young child of her own. Both her mother and father graduated from college and are teachers in a nearby city. Kendall and her family live in a middle-class neighborhood located in the same town as the school where she teaches. However, she teaches in a school that is more racially and ethnically mixed, and serves students from lower middle-class and lower-class families than her home neighborhood.

Kendall believes that all students can learn, but she knows she is not reaching every student as well as she could. She is reluctant to reconstruct her approaches, but having Parker in her classroom has motivated her to rethink her practices—especially after Parker explains that cultural competence emphasizes giving every student equitable information, access, and opportunities. Kendall realizes that she would want every teacher to provide her own child with all three elements for success.

Kendall now accepts that she needs to focus on reaching the whole child so that the teaching, learning, and schooling work together. She needs to be more attuned to her efficacy. Ready to assess her own practices so she can be a professional role model for Parker, Kendall enlists the help of her colleague Brianna, a third grade teacher, who also is a White, European American, middle-class, and married woman. Collaboratively, they develop a list of ten items that

Kendall wants Brianna to observe during Brianna's planning time. The list includes:

Locations where Kendall stands while teaching

Places she walks during work times

Length of time she stays with each student

Feedback she provides each student

Facial expressions she exhibits when talking with various students

Language she uses during conversations with various students

Posters displayed around the classroom

Examples she provides when teaching

Student centeredness of the classroom

Student involvement in the teaching and learning

Kendall and Brianna decide that Brianna will visit two or three times a week for two weeks; Brianna will select a few items each time she observes, but Kendall will not be told when Brianna will visit or which items have been selected for observation. At the end of the two weeks, Brianna will give Kendall her feedback. Kendall then plans to learn more about cultural competence from Parker as she assumes more responsibilities in the classroom.

Explore Cultural Competence 1

Cultural competence may seem like a new term to you, but it is hardly a new concept or practice. Most likely, you are acquainted with the terms *multicultural education* and *cultural diversity.* The research and conversations related to multicultural education and valuing cultural diversity have expanded and advanced to the same academic levels as all other aspects of teaching, learning, and schooling. Cultural competence embodies curricular content, instructional strategies, assessment techniques, and classroom management that all educators must know, do, believe, and respect in order to achieve efficacy.

Achieving efficacy means it is your responsibility to ensure that every student learns everything the student is expected to learn and to the best of that student's abilities. Your goal is for all students to learn about themselves as individuals, and each other as members of various groups and all of society. Every student should learn about all other students from the past, in the present, and into the future. In addition, all school families as well as all members of society should feel assured that you will fulfill your responsibilities to teach all students. Everyone is a stakeholder in you doing your job thoroughly. These outcomes can be fulfilled only through your navigation of cultural competence.

EXAMINE FAIRNESS

That's not fair. Everyone interacting with students in elementary school has heard these words. Teachers, staff, administrators, parents, and families have all encountered young students exclaiming these words or conveying the accompanying emotions through their facial expressions and body language.

Fairness embodies a sensation that each of us has experienced since early childhood. As toddlers, we acquired a meaning of fairness that seemed to be intricately involved with our entire being. From these early acquisitions, our individual views of fairness guide our cognitive thoughts, physical existence, affective emotions, and social interactions. In other words, fairness transcends all four domains of learning and influences everything we believe, think, say, and do.

Each of us developed a meaning of fairness from our parents, families, friends, and immediate communities—from the people we loved and trusted—that continued to develop with each new experience. Thus, we arrived at school with firm, yet perhaps skewed, foundations of fairness. As young children, we began to apply our individual definitions of fairness to every situation involving ourselves and the people around us. We may not have recognized or appreciated when life was fair, and we may not have comprehended the dynamics or details of each situation when fairness was questionable. Yet, we quickly understood the outcomes when we were involved, and, when warranted, we hastily articulated those three little words, *that's not fair.*

In many situations considered to be unfair, someone—frequently someone with more power and privilege, actual or perceived—has spoken or acted in ways that are judged inappropriate, unreasonable, or unkind. The words or actions may have occurred by choice or by chance. The exchanges and events may have been planned or spontaneous, direct or indirect, overt or covert; unlimited variables are associated with every situation considered as unfair. But when exchanges or events are believed to be unfair, profound short-term and long-term effects result, especially in schools and classrooms.

School administrators and classroom teachers strive to be fair in their words and actions. They teach about fairness, they manage through fairness, and they model their expectations with fairness. Yet the concept and practices of fairness often remain elusive and difficult to demonstrate for everyone at all times and in all situations. Since the ideas of fairness are contingent on cultural competence, the key to being fair is to understand cultural competence and to ensure that cultural competence is fully understood and always present.

DELVE INTO DEFINITIONS

Let's start by defining cultural competence. Culture refers to the set of shared patterns of human activity, that is, values, beliefs, and goals that characterize an individual, institution, or organization coupled with the symbolic structures that give selected activities importance. Competence involves the identified required qualities and abilities necessary for exhibiting responsibility within given contexts. Thus, cultural competence entails the knowledge, skills, dispositions, and expressions (i.e., what we know, do, believe, and respect) about ourselves, others, and society demonstrated though our thoughts, words, actions, and interactions.

For school administrators and classroom teachers in preschool and Grades K–5, practicing cultural competence equips educators with a framework for making schools more welcoming, engaging, and rewarding. When students feel safe and wanted, administrators and teachers report increased daily attendance, grade level and program completion, and academic achievement rates, along with decreased bullying, withdrawal, and dropout rates.

ESTABLISH FIRM FOUNDATIONS

Ironically, most definitions of cultural competence highlight one's abilities to interact effectively with people of different and other cultures. However, the wording of this phrase elicits several major concerns to deconstruct before you proceed. Then, you can replace your misperceptions with firmer foundations.

1. *Being different does not describe someone else; everyone is different and from a different culture.* No two people are exactly the same or share all of the same cultural characteristics; each person represents a different culture. Even brothers and sisters represent different cultures as they were raised at different times, in different context, and with different expectations.

2. *Every person is a combination of many different cultural characteristics.* One's cultural characteristics are based on nature and nurture, meaning we are born with characteristics, and we acquire characteristics by chance and by choice throughout our lives.

3. *One person's cultural characteristics are a combination of both static and dynamic cultural characteristics.* Static characteristics always stay the same (i.e., one's race or gender), and dynamic means they constantly change (i.e., one's age or education level). Therefore, foundational items 2 and 3 illustrate that a person's individual cultural characteristics are different within the person and will change over time.

4. *A person can interact effectively with other people only when a person understands his or her own individual culture and cultural characteristics.* Each one of us compares and contrasts other people with ourselves to establish our individual cultural foundation of knowledge. Only through honest self-assessments or introspections that increase awareness of ourselves can we see all of our own characteristics and self-identifiers.

5. *It is not bad to be different.* The phrase "different cultures" tends to convey that being different describes someone else and not ourselves; the phrase also infers that being different is negative, wrong, or bad. Different cultures are simply not the same cultures as the ones that currently are known and understood. And we are all different cultures.

The first five foundations emphasize your thoughts and beliefs that influence your external interactions with other people. The next five foundations focus on your internal processes that constitute your thoughts and beliefs.

6. *Each person should understand the categories and criteria used to describe one's self and thus understand and accept different cultures.* People select various words and assign various meanings to those words to describe themselves. In turn, those choices become the basis for describing and interacting effectively with other people.

7. *Each person should be aware of inward reactions toward various other people.* How one reacts to others can reveal levels of cultural competence, for all possess different cultural characteristics.

8. *Each person should be aware of outward acts toward various other people.* How one acts toward other people can influence cultural competence in others, for each of us is an influence and role model to other people.

9. *Each person, and especially teachers, should be aware of effective interactions to communicate and accomplish tasks.* Interacting effectively means something different for every person, and usually our interactions change according to the people, places, times, and events.

10. *Each person needs to be aware of one's beliefs, thoughts, words, actions, and interactions expressed in private, as well as those expressed in public—both with specific individuals and about specific individuals.* Interacting effectively in one's private thoughts means something different for every person than it does for interacting effectively in a public presence. Yet, it is said that character is who we are when we think no one is watching us.

Therefore, to interact effectively with people who are both like and unlike us, each of us must examine and understand ourselves completely to investigate our individual meanings of cultural competence, and also consider unlimited contexts and variables.

UNDERSTAND THE PURPOSE OF CULTURAL COMPETENCE

The purpose of cultural competence is to establish developmentally appropriate teaching and learning processes to ensure democratic principles, educational equity, human rights, and social justice. These four critical concepts guided the founding of the United States, and they continue to provide the framework for interacting effectively with one another formally and informally today.

1. *Democratic principles* include valuing each individual's culture and cultural characteristics, ensuring full participation in activities and decision-making procedures. Democratic principles ensure transparency, accountability, and all levels of participation from both the inside and outside of the institution.

2. *Educational equity* emphasizes that students are provided information, access, and opportunity with the necessary tools, equipment, and materials in order to learn and achieve equally to all other students. Students are taught in their languages; all students are treated with respect and dignity. Groups, schools, and institutions guarantee that all members both inside and outside the institution have their democratic principles and human rights protected.

3. *Human rights* entail the rights and freedoms that all individuals and all groups are entitled to receive and to become equal participants. Human rights include civil, political, economic, social, and cultural rights such as the right to life and liberty; the freedom of expression; equality before the law; and the right to food, work, and education.

4. *Social justice* means that all individuals and members of groups are respected and protected for their individual beliefs and choices. Teaching for social justice emphasizes antiracist and antibiased practices that deny human rights. Social justice involves interacting cooperatively and supportively to promote a common good, to end all forms of violence, to protect one another, and to take care of the planet Earth.

SET YOUR GOALS

Four goals support the overarching purpose of cultural competence (see Figure 1.1). All four involve the reciprocal process of gaining and giving:

- *Information*—to know and understand
- *Access*—to go and enter

- *Opportunities*—to do and participate
- *Respect*—to believe and value

Each of the four goals may seem quite simple and straightforward; yet, all of our beliefs, thoughts, words, actions, and interactions fit into one or a combination of the four goals. The four goals involve not only that which we receive, but they also incorporate that which we give. Every person is a part of the reciprocity in both gaining and giving information, access, opportunities, and respect.

For example, when an announcement is made that impacts an upcoming event, the people who do not receive the announcement may claim that the situation is unfair. Most likely, the announcement communicates information that one needs to know, such as that the spelling test will be given on Thursday instead of Friday. Students and their families want to know about this change so they can prepare properly. When

| Figure 1.1 | Goals of Cultural Competence |

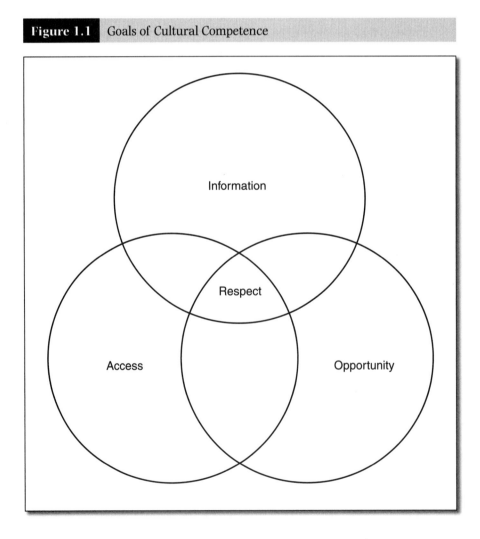

someone does not receive information, the person often is likely frustrated, and wonders, "How did other people know that?"

For some students, this change will alter their access, or whether they can prepare beforehand or go somewhere after the spelling tests are scored. For example, perhaps the teacher requires students who do not score well to write missed words repeatedly and a student who does not receive the announcement will be denied access to another event due to a lower score. The announcement thus influences opportunities or one's ability to do something. Students who receive the announcement may prepare differently than students who do not receive the announcement. In some classrooms, students who score well on their weekly spelling tests receive additional opportunities or privileges such as not being required to take a major review test. When someone is denied access, the person may be angry, and ask, "How did they get to go there or to do that?"

ENSURE RESPECT

The ultimate goal of cultural competence is to ensure respect. When someone misses an announcement and lacks information, access, or opportunities, the person responsible denies the individual respect. For example, if any students were absent when the change of date for the spelling test was announced, then these students have not been considered adequately or perhaps honored appropriately. The onus for the results of the change is transferred to the students who have to make sense of the outcomes for themselves and their families. For most students in Grades K–5, parents and family members closely monitor their children's progress in school, especially assessments such as weekly spelling test scores. Students and their families are apt to lose respect for their teachers when they do not receive the same information, access, and opportunities as other students receive.

It is easy for either a child or an adult to identify with the four purposes of cultural competence. For example, a relevant announcement could occur at a faculty meeting when you are absent. If the announcement at the faculty meeting is not posted online, distributed in writing, or shared by a colleague, you might not receive notification of a change. As a responsible educator, you are expected to investigate if you missed announcements when you are absent. However, if you cannot access the information or attain the opportunities to act upon the information, you may not receive the appropriate respect from students, families, colleagues, or administrators. Likewise, you will begin to lose respect for the individuals responsible for the situation.

So, let us modify the scenario to yet another situation that occurs frequently for adults. A change is announced with little or no input from the participants. The change causes other individuals to make significant modifications in their own plans and preparations within a short deadline, accompanied by many details and tasks. The information is shared with just a few people, presuming that "the word will get around."

Each of these scenarios compromises the four goals of cultural competence. There is inadequate information, access, opportunities, and respect. The modifications result in individuals becoming distrustful and developing perceptions that they are being treated unfairly in ways that fail to uphold democratic principles, educational equity, human rights, and social justice.

ACQUAINT YOURSELF WITH THE VOCABULARY

When denied information, access, opportunities, and respect, students may be encountering bias, prejudice, stereotyping, discrimination, marginalization, and disenfranchisement. Although people tend to use these words interchangeably, each word has a distinct definition and use.

Bias means a tendency or the inclination toward having or expressing unreasoned beliefs, thoughts, words, actions, and interactions. When someone behaves with bias, the person shows a preference for or against a particular person or a group of people based on many different actual or perceived cultural characteristics that individuals can or cannot control. Biases can be viewed as positive promotions of a person or group of persons, or negative demotions of a person or group of persons, or both.

Prejudice advances bias through preconceived and unreasoned beliefs, thoughts, words, actions, and interactions. When someone behaves with prejudice, that person has determined an opinion or outcome prior to speaking or interacting with the recipient of the prejudice. Similar to a bias, one's prejudice may be aimed at a particular person or a group of people based on many different actual or perceived cultural characteristics that individuals, again, may or may not be able to control. However, prejudicial behavior results in positive or negative outcomes that are stronger and longer lasting behaviors than biased behaviors.

Stereotyping leads to treating people, places, things, or events founded on a predetermined simplified mindset by making overgeneralizations about groups of people. Stereotyping is stronger than prejudice and serves primarily to enhance a person's power and privileges through discriminating against a group of people by denying them information, access, opportunities, and respect.

Discrimination in the positive sense means to distinguish carefully and students are taught to discriminate to identify unique qualities for positive and productive purposes. However, discrimination in the negative sense means to distinguish prejudicially. Cultural competence is denied when an individual discriminates against a person or a group of people based on a cultural characteristic—actual or perceived—and the resulting outcomes or treatments are inappropriate, unreasonable, or unkind.

Marginalization involves relegating a person or a group of people to a position of less or no power, in which the person or group has little or no participation or power. For instance, the locations of text or pictures on a piece of paper are the areas where your eyes and mind focus. The areas that seem of no consequence are the margins. When a person or group of people is marginalized, the person or group are assigned to the areas of little or no consequence or importance.

Disenfranchisement entails the deprivation or revocation of participation, position, power, or privilege that usually prevent a person or a group of people from a right. Denial of information, access, opportunities, and respect through disenfranchisement produces a stronger and longer lasting effect than marginalization.

LINK CULTURAL COMPETENCE TO LEARNING

When bias, prejudice, stereotyping, discrimination, marginalization, or disenfranchisement occur in classrooms, the absence of cultural competence significantly influences the four domains of learning: cognitive thoughts, physical existence, affective emotions, and social interactions (Gallavan, 2007). For example, a teacher may have a bias toward clean students and tend to help students who smell or appear clean more often, for more concentrated periods of time, and be more pleasant and reassuring than when assisting students who do not smell or appear as clean. Another teacher may be prejudiced against students whose parents rarely attend parent conferences, communicate with the teacher, or assist at school. This teacher may establish the same expectations for these students as the students whose parents are more visible and available and hold the students unfairly accountable for their parents' actions.

When stereotyping students, a teacher may categorize all of the girls as more quiet and calm whereas the boys are tagged as louder and busier. Therefore, the girls benefit and the boys suffer from the teacher's preconceived mindset. A teacher who marginalizes students who are overweight may spend less time and energy assisting these students. The teacher falsely associates size with ability.

Finally, students who experience disenfranchisement tend to become invisible to the teacher. English language learners and special education students are frequently the recipients of disenfranchisement. This teacher assigns the responsibility for learning to students who have been identified as needing additional intervention.

In each of these situations, the teacher limits learning in all four domains and models to the other students that some students are not equally worthy. The teacher communicates much bigger lessons to the students than the curriculum intends. Students' attitudes and behaviors frequently change due to a teacher's biases and interactions. The teacher tends to take the changes personally, not realizing that it is the teacher who has cued the student toward unpleasant and unproductive outcomes. Without honest self-assessment, teachers may or may not be aware of the words and actions preventing cultural competence.

DEVELOP YOUR SELF-EFFICACY

Navigating cultural competence requires a strong sense of self-efficacy, or your beliefs that you are capable of managing the events that influence your life (Bandura, 1997). Self-efficacy, also known as social learning theory, involves your cognitive, motivational, affective, and selection processes. Through your thoughts, actions, feelings, and choices, you increase your understanding and appreciation of achievement. You learn self-efficacy by watching others achieve success, by participating in events that culminate in success, and by being told that you are successful.

With increased self-efficacy, you increase your classroom-teacher efficacy. Your confidence and proficiency build so you can teach each student more responsibly and thus help all students increase their sense of self-efficacy. Social learning theory, as the name stipulates, is learning about ourselves, others, and society by interacting positively and productively with one another.

Social learning theory is the basis of reciprocity, or the exchange of learning and support between people. You want to identify and model reciprocity in your classroom with your students so they understand that you are learning as much from them as they are learning from you. If you are committed to developing lifelong learners, then self-efficacy, social learning theory, reciprocity, and cultural competence must be evident in your classroom every day. By learning about and with their peers, your students will exchange their academic and social outcomes with other students.

TAKE RESPONSIBILITY FOR CULTURAL COMPETENCE . . .

Practicing cultural competence is your responsibility. It is not merely a good idea or an option. You are preparing students for future learning and a long life living in a world that does not yet exist. Your task is, then, to prepare your students in every way possible. A student's time in school is short and each student's attention span is even shorter. You must maximize your teaching energies through your words and actions so that your students experience you as a role model for cultural competence as you infuse it across your curriculum content, instructional strategies, assessment techniques, and classroom management. Resource C provides a selection of websites related to cultural competence.

Extending Activities for Teachers

1. Reflect on your own learning experiences in Grades K–5. What did your teachers do and say that connected with your personal background and experiences? What did your teachers do and say that helped you feel respected and welcome? What did your teachers do and say that may have left you with feelings that you were not respected or welcome?

2. Think again to your time in Grades K–5; when did you become aware that some students were treated differently from other students? How were some students treated differently? Why did these differences occur?

3. What does the term *cultural competence* mean to you? How would you explain it in your own words, and your own example, to a colleague?

4. What can a teacher, perhaps you, do and say in a classroom to demonstrate cultural competence with young learners?

5. What should a teacher, perhaps you, avoid doing and saying in a classroom that would detract from cultural competence?

Extending Activities for Young Learners

Each of these activities should be modified for nonreaders, special education students, and English language learners as developmentally appropriate by using pictures instead of words, providing words for students to select instead of asking students to generate new words, listing possible vocabulary choices on the board, collaborating with learning assistants, and so forth.

1. Ask students to think of a word to describe themselves respectfully. The word should start with the same letter as the student's name. Then ask students to share their name combinations with a

partner. The partner will introduce the student to the class using the name combination. This activity is ideal for the first day of school.

2. Give each student a large picture of a star. Ask them to list one of their own special qualities or strengths in each of the points of the star. Students can share their stars in small group discussions. Then stars can be posted on a bulletin board or slid into a clear pocket on the front of the student's notebook. This exercise helps students recognize their individual special qualities and practice sharing their strengths with other students. This activity also is ideal for the beginning of a school year.

3. Write the word *respect* on a large sheet of paper posted on the board and discuss the meaning and actions associated with it. Ask the class to generate words and phrases that they think are appropriate for their class, and list the words and phrases under the heading. Continue adding to the list as more examples are recognized in schoolwork or class interactions. When students want to describe events that they think are examples of a lack of respect, be sure to guide the students to articulate the events as goals illustrating respect.

4. Ask students to sit in a large circle. Give each student a clipboard with a blank piece of lined paper attached to it. Ask students to print names at the top of the paper. Then have them pass their clipboards clockwise. Each student will write a few words about the student whose name is printed at the top of the sheet of paper leaving two blank lines between each entry. You may feature a few students at one sitting, and also play quiet music in the background. After all lists are written, cut the statements in the blank spaces and place the strips into an envelope labeled with each student's name. Then give students their individual envelopes at a later date and direct them to read one statement at your prompt.

5. Give each student a 3" × 5" sticky note and ask them to each record one event that they think is not fair. Then ask students to place their notes on the board or on a large piece of paper. With the class, begin to sort the notes into categories that you and the class construct together based on the information recorded on the notes. Your task is to distill the notes into a few examples. Then you and the class can discuss the examples and decide if you agree or disagree that the events were not fair. From this exercise, you and the class can determine if you can do something about the perceived lack of fairness and the action that you can take.

Elizabeth has been teaching fourth grade for nine years at the same school. Until recently, she always felt accomplished in her teaching and comfortable with her students and their families. Then the school district attendance zones were redrawn, and the student population changed in many ways. Previously, her school had a predominantly White, European American, upper-middle and middle-class, Christian and Jewish population; most students came from suburban neighborhoods with two-parent families living in houses. Elizabeth identified with her previous student population, as she is a White, European American, upper-middle-class, Christian woman married to a White, Middle Eastern, upper-middle-class, Jewish man.

The new student population has been drawn from a large tract of apartment buildings occupied by predominantly Black and Hispanic, middle- and lower-class, Christian and Muslim, primarily single-parent families. Elizabeth is anxious about the changes and knows the adjusted student population will impact her in every way.

Eager to be an effective teacher for all of her students, Elizabeth contacts her friend Alex, an Asian American man, who teaches in another school district with students and families similar to the ones who now attend her school. Elizabeth asks Alex if she can visit his classroom and talk with him about the culture of the school and community.

After spending the day with Alex, Elizabeth finds the courage to talk with him about her discomfort being around students and families unlike her. Elizabeth also shares that several new teachers have been hired at her school, all of whom are Black and Hispanic. Elizabeth reveals that she feels uncomfortable culturally with her new colleagues as well.

Alex reassures Elizabeth that, most likely, she simply has not been around many different kinds of people. Her childhood did not include a variety of cultures so she had few opportunities to develop her understanding of cultural capital.

Alex explains that cultural capital includes all of the cultural characteristics used to describe a person as an individual and as a member of various groups. The degree of capital, or value, relates to characteristics based on the sociopolitical economics of the times. For example, Elizabeth has few experiences with Black and Hispanic students and families, so she has generated limited cultural capital that she can use in her professional practices.

Alex continues by saying that perceptions associated with cultural capital are evidence of both equities and inequities generated in schools and throughout society. Teachers need to be aware of their own biases that are associated with their perceptions of cultural capital. Biases may be expressed directly (overtly) or indirectly (covertly) in what teachers say and do. Alex adds that school administrators and school board members express biases too and that Elizabeth must become aware of the dynamics to help all students and their families.

Alex shares with Elizabeth that, most likely, she is concerned that she will offend someone or embarrass herself as she accumulates her cultural capital. He tells her not to avoid people and urges her instead to approach situations based on the shared purpose and let the relationship evolve naturally.

Alex also reflects on his own experiences and how he uses "teacher self-talk." He pretends that he is teaching his learning experiences and units of learning to himself. He checks to see that the classroom environment feels safe and welcoming. He asks if he can clearly identify with the curriculum and see himself in the textbook, materials, and resources. He notes if the instruction invites him into the learning process and actively engages him to learn about himself, other people, and society. He looks for opportunities in the instruction for making meaningful connections to his personal background and experiences, and for the forms of assessment to showcase his accomplishments in ways in which he is confident.

Initially, Elizabeth believes that Alex may have more insight given that he is an Asian American; then, Elizabeth realizes that Alex's journey is the same path that all culturally competent teachers must travel.

Begin Your Transformation

2

A s you increase your knowledge and awareness for navigating cultural competence, there are some recommended steps to strengthen your transformation. Like all other change processes, you will build upon your past to understand the present and prepare for the future.

Learning about cultural competence will present opportunities to assess your current knowledge, practices, and beliefs. Then, you can develop your plans for modifying your approaches so your curricular content, instructional strategies, assessment techniques, and classroom management are more fair and inclusive. Each step in the transformation is important and supports all other steps.

APPRECIATE THE CHANGE PROCESS

Often, it seems like everybody wants things to be different, but nobody wants to change. The change process may seem more threatening than the actual change. Frequently, assessing what is happening in the present may reveal that you do not have many changes awaiting you. Then you may realize that with a few changes, you can make a big difference for you, your students, their families, and your colleagues.

The change process entails taking stock of your current situation. As each new chapter addresses a different aspect of cultural competence, reflect on the following points:

- What you know
- What you do
- What you believe
- What you value
- What you want to learn
- What you want to change

Identifying and articulating your aspirations either in a journal or to a colleague will help you hear your words and to make meaning of them. It seems easy to say that we want to be the best teachers possible, but what does that mean for each of us? The first step in the change process related to cultural competence is to specify clearly what you know, do, and believe, followed by what you want to know, do, and believe.

BE YOURSELF AND STAY OPEN

The first step in the transformation that accompanies navigating cultural competence is to be yourself. This process is lifelong, as society is dynamic and ever changing. As you encounter new people and events, hopefully your circle of knowledge and awareness continues to expand and grow. Ideally, you enter new situations by suspending your prior conceptions and acquiring a sense of openness.

Being yourself requires you to assess three dimensions: certainty, source, and structure (Schommer, 1990). Certainty entails how sure an individual feels about the knowledge one possesses. Certainty can be both liberating and limiting. Certainty is liberating when an individual feels sure that change is constant and one must be willing to stay open. Certainty is limiting when an individual feels sure that obstacles reducing freedoms accompany change. Source traces the information or supply of information to its origination. Each of us places a degree of trust and reliability into our sources of information. Structure correlates to the amount of importance the knowledge places on the way we each operate and depend on the knowledge to provide the frame for the way we function.

To think about the roles that certainty, source, and structure play on your navigation of cultural competence, imagine each criterion on a continuum (see Figure 2.1), and then rate your development (Sleeter, 2009). If you view cultural competence as achieving a singular outcome, with one right or best approach based on advice from experts, or you believe that you are doing more in your classroom because you have to rather than because you want to, you are probably a novice.

If you want to infuse cultural competence and you realize how cultural competence links multiple outcomes to multiple approaches—ones you have tailored to your students' needs and interests, and melded with your pedagogical insights and imagination—you are probably developing.

If you accept that navigating cultural competence comprises the center of teaching, learning, and schooling with uncertainty as a certainty, along with unlimited and dynamic sources, you are probably more accomplished. Your vision of cultural competence allows each student to take ownership of the learning through culturally responsive pedagogy (Gay, 2000).

| Figure 2.1 | Cultural Competence Continuum |

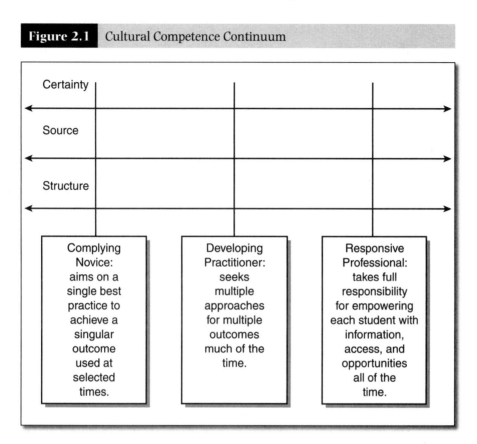

FRAME YOUR QUESTIONS

Assessing one's certainty, sources, and structure frequently generates seven areas of inquiry that influence one's transformational process (Cochran-Smith, Davis, & Fries, 2004). From your own perspectives, reflect on each of these areas:

1. *Problems and expectations:* What problems are associated with valuing diversity and achieving cultural competence in schools and society? What preconceived expectations do you have regarding how schools and society should operate?

2. *Backgrounds and beliefs:* What ideological background should teachers examine and understand in navigating one's cultural competence? What are your beliefs and dispositions about valuing cultural diversity?

3. *Knowledge and skills:* What knowledge and skills should teachers possess for cultural competence in the classroom? What content information is needed in each subject area?

4. *Content and management:* How should cultural competence be infused into classrooms as content and skills? How should cultural competence be a part of classroom management?

5. *Outcomes and evidence:* What outcomes should be taught and achieved for students to demonstrate their proficiency with cultural competence? How should outcomes be demonstrated?

6. *Preparation and accountability:* What knowledge, skills, and dispositions do teachers need to know, do, and believe to help all students excel? How should teachers be held accountable for demonstrating these proficiencies?

7. *Communities and connections:* What aspects of cultural competence are valuable for students to learn about life, connecting classrooms with communities? How should proficiency of these expectations be demonstrated in the classroom?

COPE WITH DISEQUILIBRIUM

Your responses to the seven questions about certainty, sources, and structure may generate a sense of disequilibrium or confusion (Bergeon, 2008). Perhaps you are unsure of what the best practices are for navigating cultural competence. Perhaps what you have learned in your past is incongruent with what you are learning now, and how you think schools should operate. You are beginning to realize that many home environments are not like school environments; you are also beginning to realize why many students are not successful or satisfied with school.

As you read this text, continue to consider these seven areas of inquiry. Ultimately, you want to reconcile your disequilibrium as you plan your curricular content, instructional strategies, assessment techniques, and classroom management. Your goal is to offer your students the best classroom community and educational outcomes possible.

DEMYSTIFY "DEALING WITH DIVERSITY"

First, two phrases need to be demystified and removed from conversations related to cultural competence. The first phrase is "dealing with diversity." Topics and issues related to multicultural education and diverse populations became the focus of education rather suddenly during the later half of the twentieth century. The emphasis was embraced yet seemed surprisingly ironic for some educators. Historically, U.S. schools and classrooms have always taught children from all around the world. The United States has always been a country of immigrants representing all countries, races, ethnicities, religions, governments, and so forth. People have always brought and shared many different customs, traditions, and languages.

Since it was founded, the U.S. population has been one of many different cultures, yet for centuries, the attitude was one of *assimilation,* where all new citizens would become like the dominant members of society in order to be accepted and successful. The metaphor found in most U.S. history textbooks was the United States as a melting pot; everyone would become the same.

Over time, many people concentrated on transforming this attitude so each citizen was accepted and treated equally. Laws were changed; behaviors were modified. The metaphor of a melting pot was replaced with more appropriate metaphors such as a kaleidoscope, a quilt, and a tossed salad. In each of these metaphors, the individual contributions are recognized and appreciated.

During the 1980s and 1990s, educators suddenly realized that the country's demographics were changing rapidly, prompting schools and classrooms to change too. The term *diversity* was adopted to address demographics. However, the tendency was for educators to use the term as a reference to students who were not from the dominant society. In addition, since students not from the dominant society were different, they experienced challenges in schools and classrooms that were designed for students from the dominant society; the new students were designated to the category labeled "diverse." Educators were required to modify their approaches, so educators felt forced to "deal with diversity." The term acquired a negative overtone that continues to resonate through schools and classrooms.

Perhaps the phrase "deal with" evolved simply as an alliteration as educators began to make changes; however, "deal with diversity" rarely denotes positive or productive events. Think about how you use the phrase "deal with." One never "deals with" anything that is wonderful, satisfying, or rewarding. As adults, we do not say, "I need to deal with receiving an award at work," or, "I get to deal with an extra week of paid vacation." We use the phrase "deal with" if the outcome is unwelcomed, difficult, or challenging. We might say, "I need to deal with a flat tire," or, "I get to deal with an extra bill to pay."

We must therefore stop using the phrase "dealing with diversity." Diversity cannot be unwanted; each of us is diverse. We certainly can and should value diversity so everyone is welcomed and welcomed equally.

Educators need to provide for each learner's needs and interests based on the learner's individual background, knowledge, and experiences. Students should not be grouped according to criteria that are not related to their learning. If educators have a purpose for categorizing and identifying students according to a cultural characteristic (i.e., race, gender, language, social class, and so forth), then the category should be specific and have a specific purpose. The general term *diversity* should be not used as a euphemism for race or class.

RETHINK BEING "PC"

The second phrase that needs to be demystified tends to be posed as a question. During all kinds of conversations, students and colleagues will ask, "Do I have to be PC?" Several demonstrative gestures usually accompany the question. People will wave quotation marks in the air (like rabbit ears) as they overly enunciate the initials PC, seemingly with disdain. They also are inclined to wiggle from side to side, performing the "PC dance."

Then I shock the inquirer with my reply. I gently nod my head up and down as I smile and tell them with reassurance, "Yes, you need to be PC." After the inquirer's mouth closes in disbelief, I explain that, although the world has come to assume that PC means politically correct, I have usurped the initials PC to mean other phrases that are beneficial for navigating cultural competence.

Being politically correct means one says or does something primarily for someone else. The words or actions are expressed to satisfy or placate another person or persons representative of a group or institution. The words or actions seem to be expected regardless if the individual agrees with or supports the outcomes. Many people, especially teachers, have experienced the sensation of needing to be PC.

Conversely, I encourage students and colleagues to be PC in many other ways. To be PC means they should be personally conscientious, professionally competent, and pedagogically constructive. Educators should also be publicly caring and politically concerned. Once the initials PC are demystified, students and colleagues also smile with their newfound empowerment, ready to face their own audiences.

MEET "NORMA" OR "NORMAN" AND "ABBY" OR "ABNER"

You may be wondering how and why teachers do not realize when they prevent cultural competence and limit their own efficacy. Teachers, after all, are taught to be fair and objective. However, fairness and objectivity involve a huge amount of subjectivity. Teachers simply cannot remain neutral and outside of the learning. The classroom is not a laboratory of inanimate, static objects; classrooms are filled with living, dynamic individuals. In this laboratory, the teacher is both a participant and an observer.

Every teacher always works with two invisible companions. These companions have names that are both female and male so you can identify with the ones of your choice. The first companion is "Norma" or "Norman," who encompasses the teacher's mindset of everything considered normal. While we can label things as normal based on quantitative measures, normal is far more a qualitative attribute. Also, each one of us has developed a sense of normal based on our own childhood backgrounds and individual experiences that continue to develop over time. Norma and Norman's favorite saying is "That's the way we (I) have always done it."

The other companion that works with every teacher is "Abby" or "Abner," who comprises the teacher's mindset of everything considered abnormal or not normal. Unfortunately, abnormal tends to surprise and amaze teachers. Although trying (or claiming) to maintain fairness and objectivity, too often teachers revert to their own descriptions of Norma or Norman and everything that is not considered normal is considered abnormal—and perhaps wrong or unwanted.

From the messages picked up as small children and the journeys in becoming professionals, teachers develop their own sense of normal and abnormal. Teachers learn from the modeling they observe in their own teachers, the methods they attain from their professors and cooperating teachers as interns, the mentoring they receive from their colleagues, the mandates dictated by the state, and the mission they have chosen to guide them. These six influences shape teachers' meaning of fairness, their objectivity, and, ultimately, their cultural competence (see Figure 2.2).

UNDERSTAND HERMENEUTIC PHENOMENOLOGY

All people constantly interpret and construct meaning out of the world around them. Each person's interpretation is based on unique and collective experiences extending from the individual's interactions with family, friends, colleagues, and new acquaintances associated with one's homes, education, employment, reaction, and other events. One's interpretations tend to simplify beliefs stemming from both isolated and repeated experiences, as well as stories handed down through the generations. The experiences and stories may or may not be logical and objective, yet each person is attached to individual beliefs, and the beliefs become the basis of one's reality.

This process is called *hermeneutic phenomenology* (Van Manen, 1997) and provides the description of an individual's beliefs, the justification for the words and actions associated with an individual's beliefs, and the significance that individuals place on their beliefs. Hermeneutic phenomenology

Figure 2.2 Six Major Influences on One's Meaning of Fairness

accounts for the misunderstanding and miscommunication connected especially with teaching and learning.

Each teacher constructs individual meanings of the world by comparing and contrasting that which is new and unknown to the teacher with that which is established and known to the teacher. However, the tricky part is realizing that established and known beliefs are also interpretations. In other words, every teacher constructs an individualized vision of teaching and learning from personal experiences and creates a classroom that fulfills this individual vision.

Some interpretations and resulting manifestations are appropriate and beneficial; conversely, some interpretations and manifestations are not, especially when the interpretations and manifestations relate to cultural competence. For example, a third grade teacher may believe that female students are stronger readers than male students. The teacher is female and this generality applied to her; she was a stronger reader than most of her male friends. This analysis also applied to the females and males in her family. Additionally, she has heard and read that female third graders tend to be stronger readers than male third graders. So, over time, the belief becomes the teacher's reality. From her interpretation, she unknowingly establishes different expectations for her female and male readers; her expectations tend to regulate her pedagogical approaches. This teacher may lower her standards for the male students or act upon her beliefs in ways that do not support her male students.

Teachers' beliefs are evident in their curricular development, instructional strategies, assessment techniques, and classroom management. Most people can recall a teacher who seemed biased against a particular student or group of learners. The teacher's behaviors cannot be analyzed, since the behaviors stemmed from the teacher's interpretations and constituted the teacher's individually constructed meaning in a social context. Since school is a social event, all learners are subject to each teacher's constructed meanings (Oakes & Lipton, 1999).

Teachers therefore need to be aware of their thoughts, beliefs, words, actions, and interactions. You cannot rid yourself of the presence of hermeneutic phenomenology. It is important to pose questions of yourself related to your cultural competence, then reflect upon your practices in writing. Examine your recorded notes for links to theory and research. Consider the overall interpretation and intent balanced against the specific conversations and interactions. To analyze the sense of fairness, position yourself as a recipient of your words and actions. Watch for reoccurring themes evident in your reflections, then share your notes and interpretations with a trusted mentor.

Your circle of insight will expand as you begin to view your actions and listen to your words more carefully. As you conduct new interpretations, you will compare and contrast your newly constructed meanings and, ultimately, experience change in your classroom effectiveness.

FOLLOW THE GALLAVAN CULTURAL COMPETENCE COMPASS

To guide teachers in developing their cultural competence, the Gallavan cultural competence compass (see Figure 2.3) provides eight points for navigation, with each point providing a key concept to effectively and efficiently navigate Grade K–5 classrooms.

To read the Gallavan cultural competence compass, start your orientation by looking at the north. N stands for "Notice culture and cultural

Figure 2.3 Gallavan Cultural Competence Compass

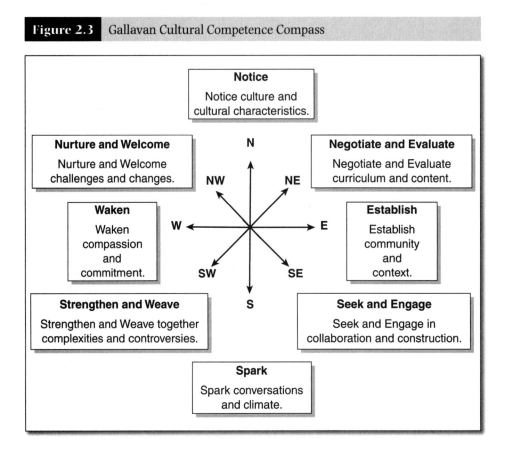

characteristics." This point emphasizes the importance of recognizing all the parts of a person in ways that are fair and objective. For example, you have most likely heard the phrase, "I don't see color" when referencing a person's racial identity. However, to be culturally competent, you are encouraged to see color and be aware of a person's cultural characteristics in totality.

To recognize other people's cultural characteristics, you must first know your own. It is critical to denote the cultural characteristics that are both like and unlike your own and to keep your two constant companions, Norma/Norman and Abby/Abner, in check. These concepts and practices are particularly critical for teachers in Grade K–5 classrooms as they design curriculum, assign instruction, align assessments, and establish a community of learners.

Moving clockwise, the next point on the cultural competence compass, NE, guides teachers to "Negotiate and Evaluate curriculum and content." Most teachers in Grade K–5 classrooms construct their own curriculum and prepare the content to meet the needs and interests of their students and the school. To ensure cultural competence, teachers must read the curricular standards and academic expectations carefully while selecting resources and materials so all students can identify with the subject matter, and apply it to their individual growth and development.

Moving clockwise, the point identified by E on the compass guides teachers to "Establish community and context." Most teachers in Grade K–5 classrooms accept this responsibility as they teach one set of students throughout most of the school day. However, many teachers in these grades may not fully understand the many different aspects associated with establishing a community context where all students feel safe and welcomed. Teachers must employ strategies for students to engage equitably in all activities, learn about themselves and one another comfortably, and find satisfaction and reward in their academic achievement.

The SE point on the compass prompts teachers to "Seek and Engage in collaboration and construction." Frequently, teachers in Grade K–5 classrooms work on grade level teams and they share ideas so all of the team members operate more efficiently and effectively. Collaboration and construction do not always occur. This point on the compass invites teachers to increase their awareness of and involvement with colleagues and agencies so that teachers can truly collaborate to construct curriculum and expand content; that is, the content and curriculum teaches all students about all other students in ways that achieve excellence, engagement, and equity.

Halfway around the compass is the S point, encouraging teachers to "Spark conversations and climate." Classrooms that demonstrate cultural competence are facilitated by teachers who set a tone that invites and encourages students to make observations, ask questions, and exchange ideas with one another. Students in Grade K–5 classrooms are just starting to express their own insights and differentiate between facts and opinions. Teachers pique students' curiosities, stimulate possibilities, and arrange opportunities for students to talk with other people like and unlike themselves. The classroom climate is one that is standards based yet student centered.

The next point on the compass is SW, where teachers "Strengthen and Weave together complexities." Cultural competence integrates the curriculum instruction, and assessment, with the best part of schooling: learning about ourselves. Anytime we learn about ourselves, we encounter the complexities and controversies of life. This point on the compass allows classrooms to delve into topics and issues that capture students' attention. Examining complexities and exploring controversies empowers students with a sense of adulthood and importance.

Moving clockwise, the next point on the compass leads to W, "Waken compassion and commitment." This point accompanies the SW point and many other points. When opening conversations related to controversies, the culturally competent teacher must skillfully tie discussions together with compassion and commitment. When probing how people are the same and different, the teacher must instill dispositions of kindness and concern that are genuine and long lasting. Students need guidance in developing an in-depth acuteness about people and for giving people their attention. Too often, teachers organize a service learning project, yet it minimizes feelings of compassion and commitment.

Closing the circle around the compass brings us to NW, where we "Nurture and Welcome challenges and changes." This point is one of the most difficult for both children and adults. Most people try to cope with challenges and avoid too many changes, especially at one time. Cultural competence requires students and teachers to stay open to challenges, and to view challenges as opportunities to become involved in situations and to make a positive difference with compassion and commitment. Change is a constant and teachers should think about ways to help their students through critical thinking, decision making, and problem solving so that challenges and changes are readily accepted.

CONNECT WITH CULTURALLY RESPONSIVE PEDAGOGY

Achieving cultural competence in your classroom requires using culturally responsive pedagogy. Here are six strategies that should be visible in your classroom:

1. *Speak the language(s) of your students.* When students are bilingual, use as much of the native language as possible. Encourage all students to begin speaking all languages.

2. *Engage students in their own learning.* Create learning experiences in which students must use critical thinking, decision making, and problem solving in contexts that are meaningful to individual students.

3. *Place all learning in both individualized and shared contexts through examples and stories.* Encourage students to share their own examples and stories so that students learn from one another.

4. *Organize projects so that students work in cooperative learning groups.* Students need structured opportunities to work effectively with other people to construct a single outcome as a cohesive team.

5. *Extend the learning through individually selected readings and projects.* When each student reads a different text or constructs a different outcome, the various texts and outcomes can be shared in class so that students learn more knowledge and skills from the multiple perspectives of their peers.

6. *Develop thematic units of learning so learning is natural, authentic, and holistic.* You can cover much more material by combining expectations thoughtfully; students will make stronger connections when outcomes reinforce one another.

ACT NOW . . .

To help get you started on your travels with cultural competence, you are encouraged to ACT NOW. This is an acronym created to help you remember the process:

Acknowledge the past. Everyone's story is a part of history. Although some people may claim that to include everyone's story is to rewrite history, resulting in far too much history to learn, you can promote cultural competence by being knowledgeable of a more complete story, and acknowledging the individuals who can help tell a more complete story; this way, everyone can be in the story.

Confront the present. The word *confront* may seem harsh or hostile, yet it is chosen by design. Confront means to meet head-on to face the situation. In order to fully understand today's world and relationships, you and your students must confront the present conditions.

Transform the future. Acknowledge the past and confront the present to empower yourself and your students to transform the future. Based on the history of the United States, we know this pattern has been effective. Every positive change has followed the same pattern, and these are important patterns for today's students in sixth through twelfth grade classrooms to learn, practice, and become competent.

Navigate the scene. As you steer the transformation in your classroom, use the cultural competence compass to navigate each day or scene. Rely on the eight points to orient yourself and guide you.

Own the situation. Teachers have been afforded the wonderful situation of being in control of their own classrooms. As you navigate cultural competence, take ownership of the change to ensure democratic principles, educational equity, human rights, and social justice occur with every opportunity.

Work the solution. No situation will be solved and stay solved. You have to continue working the situation to ensure cultural competence through your own professional growth and development. Then, you can work with your students, their families, and your colleagues and introduce the Gallavan cultural competence compass.

Resource C provides a selection of websites related to cultural competence.

Extending Activities for Teachers

1. Think about your (current or future) classroom in terms of cultural competence. What certainties can you identify that pertain to your classroom? How are you sure of the items that you have labeled as certainties?

2. Continuing the reflection in the first activity, what are the sources of the certainties? How well do you trust your sources?

3. Then, how do your certainties and sources influence the structures upon which your classroom is built? How confident are you that these structures are serving you and all of your students well?

4. How open are you to new ideas related to your classroom? Are you more open to instructional strategies than to ideological beliefs? How can you blend your thoughts and beliefs so they are constructive for more students?

5. Look on the Internet for ideas related to extending cultural competence beyond the classroom through social action or service learning projects. Consider one or two ideas in terms of your degree of certainty, source, and structure. Are you open enough to add a culturally competent service learning project to your curriculum?

Extending Activities for Young Learners

Each of these activities should be modified for nonreaders, special education students, and English language learners as developmentally appropriate by using pictures instead of words, providing words for students to select instead of asking students to generate new words, listing possible vocabulary choices on the board, collaborating with learning assistants, and so forth.

1. Place students in groups, and ask each group to name one idea that is certain for them. Explore the concept of checking one's understanding of certainty by asking students to list questions to check their certainty. Share the questions to model the importance of inquiry.

2. Practice the change process with your students concentrating on each step. Create a reasonably fictitious situation about which you anticipate your students care and would like to change. Start by

asking them what they know and record their responses. Then ask them what they believe, and again record their responses. At this point, it is essential to help them differentiate between their thoughts and feelings. Then, proceed with asking them what they want to change, why they want to make changes, and how they can make changes. Emphasize how people need to examine their thoughts and feelings before leaping into making changes.

3. As a large group, discuss the concept of normal by drawing a large circle that represents one individual. For this exercise, the individual is fictitious. Ask the students to contribute characteristics about this individual (e.g., boy, Hispanic, third grade, mom and dad, two sisters, grandmother, baseball player, and so forth). Highlight that this is what the fictitious character, or boy, thinks is normal. Then, draw another circle around the outside of the first circle. Identify characteristics that might be considered abnormal for this fictitious character. Then imagine, as a whole group, the characteristics that might become normal. This discussion should demonstrate that each of us has a different definition of normal and abnormal, with everything ultimately falling into normal.

4. Ask students to journal privately about a time that they had to work or play with someone who they did not know and did not believe they would like until they started working or playing together. The journal entries should include the events and changes that occurred in the relationship. Then invite students to share their entries or to describe the events.

5. In a large room or outside, provide each student with a compass and introduce the four primary directions and four intermediary directions. Ask students to walk a specific number of steps in a specific direction to learn how to follow a compass. This activity teaches students that there are different directions to travel, to follow directions, and perhaps to enter one another's "space." This activity also allows students to go outside and move around with one another.

Justin is a new fifth grade teacher and feels ready to teach the curriculum. He successfully completed his internship working with an accomplished fifth grade teacher in the same school building, and therefore knows he can go to his colleague for help at any time for mentoring. However, after a few weeks of school, Justin realizes that he is not connecting as easily with his students as his mentor, Nathan, connects with his students. After school one day, Justin meets with his mentor seeking guidance.

Nathan asks Justin to tell him what Justin sees when he looks at his students. Justin and Nathan are both White, European American, middle-class men. Justin is engaged and Nathan has been married for twenty-five years, with children the same age as Justin.

Justin describes the students in terms of their learning abilities and levels of cooperation. Nathan probes the question further, inquiring about the students' genders, races, ethnicities, socioeconomic situations, and native languages. Nathan asks Justin what he knows about his students' families and homes and to identify students who live in houses versus apartments; students who live with one parent, two parents, or grandparents; students with siblings and without siblings; and finally, students who go to day care before and after school, go home after school, have part-time jobs, or are involved in clubs and sports.

Justin admits that he does not possess this knowledge about his students. He offers the weak explanation that he has been busy getting to know his students academically and maintaining classroom control. Nathan confirms that Justin is starting appropriately and professionally, and now, it is time to see his learners in their entirety. That means Justin must notice each learner as a person in order to navigate culture competence.

Nathan tells Justin that he will benefit by recognizing that he is receiving and organizing stimuli all the time. Nathan continues kindly, adding that most people are unaware of the encounters and events occurring around them until the individual either becomes frustrated or someone becomes frustrated with the individual, such as Justin now experiences. Nathan suggests that Justin begin the processes of transforming himself from being naive to starting to notice the world around him.

Nathan explains that people have multiple ways or receptors for noticing the world—through one's senses, through one's thoughts or sensibilities, and through one's feelings or sensitivities. This means that Justin must take some time to acknowledge what he detects with each of his senses, thoughts, and feelings in order to detect patterns of what he notices and what he misses. With analyses, Justin can probe the possible causes accounting for either his acknowledgment or oversight of various stimuli. Only then will he begin noticing much more of the world around him, and the ways that everyone fits and functions within it.

Justin asks Nathan why he has not noticed the world around him as fully as Nathan sees it. Nathan continues that Justin, and most people, are products of their homes and communities. Justin notices what other people noticed and acknowldged. Nathan predicts that once Justin begins to notice and analyze the items he notices, his teaching as well as his life will become richer, fuller, and more interesting.

N: Notice Culture and Cultural Characteristics　**3**

The first point on the Gallavan cultural competence compass starts with the letter N for "Notice," highlighting the significance for your reading this book and reflecting on your teaching. To notice means to become aware, perceive, and recognize all forms of input around you.

In order to notice everything in your classroom, there are three steps to follow. First, establish a *focus* so you can concentrate completely. This means you have to comprehend what you notice and what you do not notice. In order to absorb everything, you may need to force yourself to notice everything within an environment several times.

Second, create *filters* to control the many different pieces of information and stimuli that are constantly bombarding you; then you can continue to strengthen the focus in step one. For example, if you want to maximize your focus on one student in your classroom, then you must minimize your attention to other students. Understandably, a teacher must be aware of everything and everyone in the classroom; however, in order to fully notice, you will have focus and filter.

Finally, manage the *findings*, or the items that you notice, allowing you to create purpose, increase your productivity, and discover pleasure for yourself and the people around you. Discerning all aspects of your observation allows you to rationalize meaning or a purpose for each discovery. The aim is to increase your attentiveness so you can concentrate on situations, and subsequently apply the findings at appropriate times and in suitable places.

Everyone and everything that you notice in your classroom relates to culture and cultural characteristics (Banks, 2008). After all, you are a human being, you are teaching human beings, and you are teaching *about* human beings. This chapter guides you through processes for, and importance of, noticing the culture and cultural characteristics of human beings, especially the students in your classroom. Activities at the end of the chapter help you learn more about yourself and provide ideas for you to also guide your young learners in noticing culture and cultural characteristics.

ACCOUNT FOR SENSES, SENSIBILITIES, AND SENSITIVITIES

To notice illuminates a multifaceted action involving an individual's senses, sensibilities, and sensitivities. Through our five physical senses we hear, see, smell, taste, and touch. From our sensibilities, we think by drawing upon prior knowledge to engage in problem solving. Also with our sensitivities, we feel by releasing our emotions. Using each of these multiple forms of input to understand the world and to map our travels may seem direct, logical, and easy, as if each person's perceptions about other people and events are all the same all the time.

However, people are not robotic machines, and our senses, sensibilities, and sensitivities do not operate with clarity, objectivity, or standardization. We do not generate the same perceptions about all people and events all the time. And, to add to the complexity, our own individual perceptions are inconsistent; we don't even generate the same impression about any one person or event every time.

The five senses found in each person vary in physical strength and accuracy; likewise, brain functions and emotional expressions range in each of us. Combining one's senses, brains, and emotions creates an individual with unique features and special qualities who is both alike and unlike other people. There are similarities and differences in how each of us perceives ourselves, one another, and all situations. To complicate the situation, each of us tends to select, prioritize, and categorize all the forms of input we receive, based on our education and experiences, including the six major influences on our meaning of fairness and cultural competence introduced in Chapter 1.

EXAMINE SENSATIONS

Our senses contribute significantly to how we notice the world around us. People rely upon each of the five senses to function independently and in unison with one another and a total unit. If you are like most people, you rarely think about each of your five senses in isolation unless one of them is not functioning well. When one of your five senses is limited, either temporarily or permanently, you attune much more to the loss. Then, you may seek ways to compensate for the loss.

Although each of the senses performs a particular function, people do not use any one of the five senses fully. Perhaps the human brain has not developed so people can recognize everything that the senses detect. However, each of us has developed patterns associated with each sense.

Consider your eyesight. There are two sayings, in particular, that apply to vision. The first tells us that we tend to see what we want to see. As you walk through familiar settings such as your home, what do you see? Most people will see what they are seeking. So, if you are looking for your car keys, you concentrate on the places where your car keys might be. However, if you are analyzing the color of your walls throughout your house, you concentrate on the color scheme flowing from one room to another room. You readjust your visual scope and acuity based on the purpose.

Now transfer your visual awareness to the classroom and its impact on your cultural competence. What do you see? What do you seek? What do you want or hope to see? What do you want or hope not to see? Do you see everything that is happening (even though teachers do not have eyes in the backs of their heads)? Or do you see only what you want to see?

Let's now consider the second saying. This tells us that it is not so much that we believe what we see; it is that we tend to see what we believe. Now ask yourself, what do you want to see? What do you want to believe that you see? It is imperative that you assess your visual scope and acuity.

In the classroom, these same types of questions and concerns apply to your sense of hearing. What do you hear? What do you want and hope to hear? What do you want and hope not to hear? Again, we teasingly associate a heightened sense of hearing with most teachers. Yet, once more, it is imperative that you assess your hearing scope and acuity.

It may seem that the scope and acuity associated with your senses of smell, taste, and touch would not impact your effectiveness in the classroom as much as your sense of seeing and hearing. However, each sense contributes to your cultural competence. Do you notice smells emanating from each student? What does each smell make you think? How does each smell make you feel? Do you associate particular smells with particular beliefs? Are your associated beliefs accurate? Fair? Necessary?

What is the impact when students describe various types of food? Consider what you think and how you feel. Ask yourself about this when students describe how something feels when it is touched. Although you may not actually taste or touch the same items, your brain and emotions elicit memories so you think you have replicated the same experience.

Most likely, you have not generated the same sensations or experiences through any of your five senses. You are a different person physically, mentally, emotionally, and socially. You come from another place, time, and background. Although people frequently reference a sensation as a universal experience, you simply cannot presume that any two people manifest the same impressions from any sensation.

DECONSTRUCT THINKING

Your brain greatly affects the scope and acuity you associate with each sensation. Both nature and nurture contribute to the sensation (in isolation and combination with other sensations), the strength and clarity of the sensation, and, most important, the message that the sensation elicits. You were born with natural abilities that served you immediately. You were also born with potential abilities that you have developed throughout your lifetime.

However, you were not born with the words and meanings for your sensations. The people around you have informed you from the first day. Someone else has told you—through speaking, listening, and reading— the names used to identify and describe all the things that you see, hear, smell, taste, and touch. As you have grown, you have encountered new environments and situations that expanded your established knowledge and introduced new knowledge. Hopefully, you will forever be receptive to new thoughts associated with your sensations.

Thinking is not and cannot be objective, no matter how hard we try and ask of our students. No two people are born with the same sensors; people's sensors do not maintain their strength and accuracy as we mature. Most languages offer an abundance of words used to identify and describe objects cognitively. Think of all the communication challenges we each encounter every day. The dilemma centers on balancing common and expressive language to articulate unlimited sensations experienced by billions of individuals.

ANALYZE EMOTIONS

In addition to your senses and sensibilities, your sensitivities known as your emotions or feelings also significantly impact you. You interpret the world in your own unique way. Your emotions or feelings are highly subjective and easily influenced by everything occurring around you and inside you.

Although difficult if not impossible to trace, your emotions or feelings tend to overpower your sensibilities or thinking when interacting with other people. For example, when you see a person you may think or presume that you are thinking about the individual almost objectively if you were to describe the person. However, your emotions elicit feelings that tend to assign values and beliefs to your sensations and thinking so they become more subjective.

Most likely, you are not even aware of the power that your assumptions, values, and beliefs have on you. They have become a part of your life; they comprise what you call normal. You acquired your assumptions, values, and beliefs from the people whom you love and respect, so you might not realize you ascribe to these beliefs. Most of the time, there were few or no reasons to question them. However, as you begin to notice the people and events around you, and truly notice them, you will begin to probe the catalyst for your assumptions, values, and beliefs as well as your words, actions, and interactions that stem from them. Understandably, scrutinizing yourself may reveal discoveries that are difficult for you to understand or accept. You might also experience some resistance when you begin to notice patterns that make you uncomfortable.

RECOGNIZE SELECTIVITY

Life produces too many stimuli for you to process them all at once. Thus, through well-honed selectivity, you decide which stimuli to receive. You then categorize and prioritize the stimuli so you can function. To better know yourself, delve into these categories and priorities: Are you automatically grouping individuals and ranking them without merit?

Most likely, you have acquired processes like these that limit your cultural competence and, therefore, your ability to be an effective teacher for all of your students. For example, when you look at your classroom, whom do you see, and what do you notice about these particular students? What do you hear? Are you tapping into your senses completely so you see and hear all of your students with as much information as possible? Or through selectivity, do you see and hear only particular aspects about your students that you want to see and hear? Perhaps what you see and hear consists of only negative or unacceptable behaviors that you are compelled to address. During these times, your emotions supersede your thinking, forcing you to interact ineffectively.

CONNECT THROUGH VALUE THEORY

It is neither pleasant nor easy for anyone, especially a teacher, to admit that one's assumptions, values, and beliefs may be limiting one's cultural competence. Like most teachers, you have not been guided in making connections, and you are eager to learn so you can be effective with every student. You want to expand your abilities for your five senses to acknowledge all stimuli to fully inform your thinking. You want to see and hear what is going on around you as completely, clearly, and objectively as possible.

As you process the stimuli, check your assumptions, values, and beliefs. Do you practice selectivity in what you see and hear? Do you categorize inaccurately, unfairly, or too quickly? Do you prioritize illogically, unjustly, or excessively?

These questions are associated with value theory (Thye, 2000). This theory examines your abilities to analyze what you deem worthy and unworthy, how you prioritize your values, and why you prioritize and act upon your prioritizations. Value theory is based on empirical evidence, or the events that you acknowledge in your life everyday.

You probably know many teachers who demonstrate an absence of cultural competence. They exist by chance and by choice. Unfortunately, some teachers will either become aware or are already fully aware of their assumptions, values, and beliefs and will continue to avoid cultural competence. Their biases, prejudices, and stereotypes have become ingrained in their existence and they choose not to change. This choice harms all students. You know these teachers; they may have been your teachers. Hopefully you are committed to transforming your thoughts, feelings, words, actions, and interactions to align with cultural competence.

INVESTIGATE THE CONTEXT OF CULTURE

The word *culture* encompasses all characteristics that describe a person as an individual and as a member of many different groups. Each characteristic is considered separately and collectively, integrated with some or all other characteristics. Cultural characteristics are innate (i.e., acquired through birth) and social (i.e., learned through living). Some cultural characteristics are static, meaning an individual possesses or selects that characteristic throughout life and, in most cases, either cannot or does not change the characteristic.

Conversely, some cultural characteristics are dynamic, meaning they continue to change over time by chance, by choice, or not by choice. For example, a characteristic that changes due to chance might be changing from knowing someone to not knowing someone. By chance, two individuals meet, are attracted to one another, and develop a relationship. A characteristic that changes due to choice might be if the two individuals in this scenario decide to get married. A characteristic that changes not by choice is the two individuals growing older over time.

Eight categories of cultural characteristics are listed in Figure 3.1, in alphabetical order. No category is more or less important than another category. The examples given for each of the eight categories provide only a few illustrations and should not be considered as belonging exclusively to only one category or as being an exhaustive list of examples for the category.

Figure 3.1	Eight Categories of Cultural Competence

1. Affective emotions, such as dispositions, attitudes, and feelings.
2. Cognitive thoughts, such as knowledge, language, and intellect.
3. Group memberships, such as communities, institutions, and organizations.
4. Performance abilities, such as skills, dexterity, and talents.
5. Personal affiliations, such as art, music, and sports.
6. Physical descriptors, such as skin color, sexual orientation, and weight.
7. Social behaviors, such as interactions, communications, and relationships.
8. Spiritual beliefs, such as religion, philosophy, and well-being.

Although eight categories of cultural characteristics are identified in Figure 3.1, it is vital that each human being is viewed and views other human beings holistically or as the total sum of all the parts. This idea is extremely challenging for many people to comprehend and achieve, both when describing themselves and when describing other people. The tendency is to fixate on cultural characteristics in isolation. This outcome occurs in society and in classrooms, detracting from cultural competence. For example, meet Matt. He can be described as a popular second grade boy, who reads below grade level, has brown hair and brown eyes, loves soccer, and is cocaptain of his team. In this sentence, there are descriptors that fit within each of the eight categories. However, the individual is not just one of the descriptors; Matt is a human being with many different qualities that are inextricably intertwined. There is much more for you to learn about Matt as you enhance your senses, sensibilities, and sensitivities.

EXPAND YOUR VIEW

Regardless of your view of an individual's cultural characteristics, you cannot identify all of them nor can you acquire a complete understanding of each characteristic. Each characteristic is accompanied by three levels: surface, intermittent, and deep. The commonly used metaphor of an iceberg fits here (see Figure 3.2).

Just as the visible section of an iceberg is called the surface, every cultural characteristic can be identified and described with words that people use frequently and images that people recognize quickly. Surface descriptions tend to be concrete, obvious, and familiar; the descriptions also tend to be temporary, contemporary, and based on popular culture gained from the media. References for surface characteristics are taught explicitly and are widely accepted, particularly in cross-cultural communications.

Figure 3.2 Cultural Characteristics Iceberg

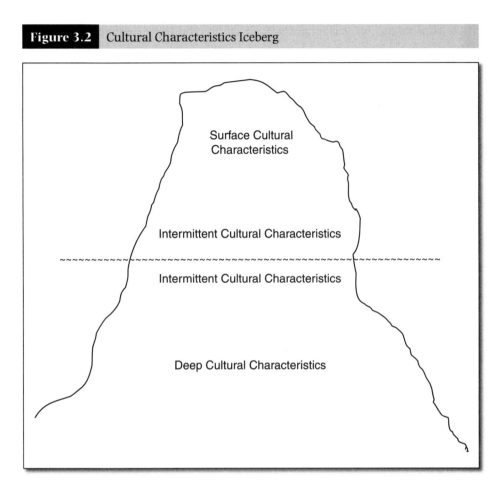

Surface Cultural
Characteristics

Intermittent Cultural Characteristics

Intermittent Cultural Characteristics

Deep Cultural Characteristics

Surface analyses account for what is seen, but they provide only the tip of the iceberg. Continuing with our example, Matt is a boy with brown hair and brown eyes who is cocaptain of the soccer team. Most likely, Matt would be identified readily among a group of second graders on the soccer field.

The intermittent, or transitional, level of an iceberg represents aspects of cultural characteristics that fluctuate in their visibility, recognition, and clarity. Symbols, meanings, and expectations are associated with the intermittent level. Intermittent descriptions tend to be vague, ambiguous, and subjective; the descriptions are contingent upon other characteristics and based on individual interpretation. References for intermittent characteristics are caught more than they are taught.

Intermittent analyses reveal the alternating and irregular explanations linked with what is meant as conveyed through language. For example, Matt reads below grade level so he does not apply himself adequately to his reading like he does playing soccer. Matt might be labeled as an underachiever.

Below the waterline of the iceberg lies the deep cultural level. Deep cultural characteristics are composed of values, beliefs, and traditions shared within a group but not understood or accepted among all people. Deep cultural characteristics address elements of time, space, and one's existence. These cultural characteristics are obscure, opaque, and difficult to detect and to describe; deep cultural characteristics usually are historical in nature, permanent pillars in a group, and hidden from public view.

Deep cultural characteristics are not gleaned from posted documents or taught directly; they tend to be passed along implicitly by group elders and learned through participation and modeling for individuals who are selected to receive instruction. For example, since Matt reads below grade level and is cocaptain of his soccer team but has brown hair and brown eyes, one might surmise that Matt will get through school based entirely on his athleticism and that his family does not possess the knowledge or techniques to help him achieve academically. The presumption may extend to believing that Matt is not worth the current investment for future opportunities.

The iceberg metaphor provides a model to cluster the patterns of labels that each of us creates and their corresponding relationships to surface, intermittent, and deep cultural connections. Realizing what, how, and why one clusters and connects cultural characteristics, and aspects of cultural characteristics, is key to every teacher's success.

DESCRIBE YOURSELF

The first step in the transformation toward cultural competence is for you to describe yourself (McIntosh, 1989). Completing this exercise will help reveal the vocabulary, concepts, and practices you possess about culture and cultural characteristics. For each of the eight categories in Figure 3.1, list words and phrases that describe you. When completing the self-description, record the first ideas that come to you. Do not contemplate too long or attempt to analyze (or overanalyze) the ideas that you record.

Try to be thorough and honest. If you are comfortable with a spouse, sibling, or friend, you might invite that individual to contribute to your list. It can be interesting to hear how someone you trust describes you, especially to help you get started. However, it is better to expand on your lists on your own; it is also imperative that you keep your list private as the lists constitute your own self-awareness and self-analysis.

Some of the descriptors will seem more objective than other descriptors that may seem more subjective. Also, various kinds of descriptors will apply to the same characteristic. For example, you may identify yourself as female, a seemingly objective descriptor. Yet you may also characterize yourself as a female intensely interested in fashion, glamour, and so forth. Perhaps you describe these characteristics as being more feminine. Remember, it is your list of descriptors.

As you unfold the many layers of your being, you will begin to identify your unique characteristics. Naturally, some of the characteristics that you associate with one of the eight categories will closely associate with another category. You are starting to view and describe yourself holistically.

CHECK YOUR REACTIONS

Now, check your reactions to the items on your list. Most likely, your discoveries will both satisfy and stymie you. You may have known and accepted that you described yourself as one particular characteristic. Yet checking your thoughts and feelings associated with that characteristic may reveal that you appear to others in a way that you did not intend or do not like. For example, continuing with our previous example, the female who described herself as being interested in fashion and glamour realized that some people may think she is superficial and feel she is silly. The female may perceive that some believe she is not intelligent and therefore she is not taken seriously at work. This female might become defensive based on her analysis, or she might recognize that she can help the people around her to understand and accept her, thus expanding cultural competence in other people.

The reverse reaction can also occur when conducting a self-description. An individual may discover that one's group memberships and social interactions are limiting one's cultural competence in understanding and accepting other people. Again, some individuals will appreciate these enlightened analyses; other individuals will become defensive, reinforcing their limited cultural competence.

PLAN YOUR TRAVELS . . .

Once you have initiated the processes of identifying your cultural characteristics and how you notice yourself, one another, and the world around you, it behooves you to identify some goals to enhance your cultural competence and introduce it into your classroom. Crafting three goals as you map your travels is a reasonable expectation. Write one goal that focuses on developing your abilities to notice augmenting your senses, sensitivities, and sensibilities. Your purpose is to recognize more events happening all around you, and the resulting thoughts and feelings.

Write another goal for interacting with just one other individual. Perhaps you have discovered from your self-description that you spend almost no time with one specific student because the student does not speak English accurately or clearly. Because it is difficult for you to understand the student, your solution—perhaps unknowingly—has been to avoid talking with the student and staying busy with other tasks. Your purpose is to get to know the student, to listen, and to learn to communicate.

Write a third goal for increasing your awareness of, and ability to, coexist within the world around you. Most people recognize there are cultural characteristics that they feel they cannot accept. Try to gain more information about the cultural characteristic; perhaps you can become acquainted with an individual representative of the cultural characteristic or visit an area where many individuals possessing this particular cultural characteristic are found. Your purpose is to expand your understanding of both the cultural characteristic and your own reactions to the sensations, thoughts, and feelings that you manifest. From these experiences, you will be able to interact with all of your students and their families with increased cultural competence, inside and outside of the classroom.

Extending Activities for Teachers

1. As you travel along your usual daily path, think about using your senses—particularly your ears, eyes, and nose—just one time when you did not use them in the past. What do you notice now? Connect the sensation that you notice with one isolated thought (not a feeling). Identify the thought and provide a rationale for the thought. Then connect to a feeling; identify the feeling and, again, provide a rationale. Is the sensation accurate? Is your thought reasonable? Is your feeling respectful? Why have you determined these particular sensations, thoughts, and feelings? Where did they originate? Finally, consider steps you can initiate to reroute the accuracy of your sensations, the reasonability of your thoughts, and the respectfulness of your feelings. The next time you travel the same route in your usual daily path, start to associate more accurate sensations, reasonable thoughts, and respectful feelings. Then notice the changes in yourself.

2. Go to a public setting, such as the mall, where you can sit and watch the shoppers for at least an hour. As you watch the shoppers, record what you notice about them both individually and as members of groups. After twenty or thirty minutes, review your notes for patterns in your observations. Then watch the shoppers for another twenty or thirty minutes, and again record your

observations. Compare and contrast your notes. From this exercise, you should be able to start analyzing what you notice. As you increase your awareness, begin to formulate a rationale for your observational patterns.

3. Visit the same mall or a different location, such as the library or airport. On a piece of paper, list the five senses. Next to each title, record what you sense (hear, see, smell, taste, and touch) in a vertical column. Then, next to each recorded sense, write if the perception is positive, negative, or neutral. When you are finished with the list, analyze your senses.

4. Create a list of your cultural characteristics. Next to each item, rate it as one that is viewed positively or negatively in society. Then, next to each rating, describe how the rating makes you feel. This exercise allows you to connect cultural characteristics, feelings, and thoughts.

5. Consider what a teacher, perhaps you, should do and say in a classroom to demonstrate cultural competence with young learners. Consider what a teacher, perhaps you, should avoid doing and saying in a classroom that would detract from cultural competence.

Extending Activities for Young Learners

Each of these activities should be modified for nonreaders, special education students, and English language learners as developmentally appropriate by using pictures instead of words, providing words for students to select instead of asking students to generate new words, listing possible vocabulary choices on the board, collaborating with learning assistants, and so forth.

1. Place each student with a partner or ask students to select a partner as appropriate in your classroom. Give each student a handheld mirror. (Some schools have classroom sets of mirrors in their math supplies for teaching symmetry.) Instruct students to observe themselves, carefully noting the placement and colors of their features. Then, provide students with all colors of construction paper that they will tear (not cut) into shapes to construct their self-portraits. (Remove the white paper, or provide white paper only for reproducing the whites of the eyes.) Encourage students to ask their partners to help them construct their self-portraits as accurately as possible.

2. Create a graphic organizer for students to list their memberships in various groups such as their family, classroom, religious organization, sports team, music group, special interests, neighborhood,

state, country, and so forth. This activity allows students to identify and see their assorted relationships.

3. Using large sheets of colorful bulletin board background paper, ask each student to lie down on a sheet of paper in the color the student chooses. Then, trace around each student's entire body, and then have students cut out their own shape. Using magazines and newspapers, next have students cut out and paste words and pictures that describe themselves onto their shapes. Completed shapes can be displayed in the students' chairs for back-to-school night.

4. Teach your students about the five senses (i.e., to hear, see, smell, taste, and touch). Discuss how people develop their senses based on education and experience. Emphasize that each person has positive, negative, and neutral preferences associated with each sense. Bring a variety of items to the classroom for students to hear, see, smell, taste, and touch. Then, ask students what each sensation makes them think and feel, highlighting reality and perceptions.

5. Design a picture of an iceberg that can be copied and distributed. Reproduce the picture of the iceberg so you have a large copy to use with the whole class. Label the three sections of the iceberg as "surface," "intermittent," and "deep." Create a list of descriptors featured among students and list them on the board. Ask students to place the words in one of the three sections of the iceberg and to be ready to explain their placements. Words to list could include appearance, gender, language, religion, favorite school subject, favorite sports team, favorite food, hobbies, least favorite school subject, fears, and so forth.

Valencia has been teaching second grade for two years in a culturally diverse, urban setting where most students tend to score on or just below average on end-of-unit assessments and state tests. Fortunately, when she was hired she joined a strong team of second grade teachers who have guided her with day-to-day instructional practices and classroom management. However, it seems to Valencia that her team skims the surface of the curriculum and expects the students to show progress even when the students do not fully comprehend the content. Frequently she overhears her team commenting that the students are just not getting it.

There are times that she, too, has felt challenged in connecting the content to her students and understanding the activities that her team of teachers uses. Like some of her students, Valencia is a White, Hispanic American woman and was raised in a single-parent home where finances were tight. Valencia wants to develop her curriculum so it is much more powerful and purposeful. She wants all parts of the curriculum to fit together smoothly and connect with the students meaningfully.

During the summer break, Valencia locates the school's mission and vision statements along with the school's goals. She makes a copy of the school calendar and highlights the major events held annually at the school. She attaches all her state standards and academic expectations to a large bulletin board so all of them are visible. Then she places each of her required textbooks on a table below the boards.

Reflecting on her first two years of teaching, Valencia realizes that her second graders seem to maintain interest in units of learning for approximately two weeks. However, even when the units are limited to two weeks in length, her students' scores tend to remain at or below average. Therefore, Valencia's motivation to reorganize her curriculum aims to fulfill two major outcomes: increasing her students' interest and increasing her students' scores for her units of learning.

After examining the collected materials, Valencia asks herself five revealing questions:

1. Why would these students want to learn this content?

2. Where do these students see themselves individually and as members of various groups in the content?

3. How do the learning activities stimulate learning for these students and connect to their immediate lives?

4. What opportunities are available for these students to express themselves in ways that best convey their accomplishments?

5. When should this content occur in relationship to the entire curriculum, instruction, and assessment plan for these students?

As Valencia begins to answer her own questions, she recognizes that her current approaches are not adequate. She surmises that her students do not connect with the curriculum as the presented content has little to do with them or their prior knowledge, and her pedagogical processes do not showcase their strengths or build upon their skills. Valencia discovers that she needs to establish context to bridge her students with the curriculum.

Probing her five questions forces Valencia to view the classroom through the perspectives of her students and their families. In order for her students to connect with the curriculum, she must be sure the curriculum includes them. Valencia likes to organize her units of learning based on social studies and science, so she guides her school-year map based on these academic disciplines. She lists the topics she must cover and sequences them so one topic leads logically into the next topic. Now she can build upon prior knowledge and skills with confidence that her students have demonstrated interest and proficiency.

Valencia also starts a second list of topics that parallels the first list. This second list identifies topics that she wants to integrate into the state curriculum. She lists various individuals' names along with local, regional, national, and global events that relate to the topics but are not included in the curriculum or textbooks. Now Valencia is infusing cultural competence into her curriculum. She is taking important steps in her curriculum mapping to tell a more complete story, infusing individuals and events the students and their families may know. Valencia realizes that she will have to do her own homework to enrich the content, but she is excited that her efforts will attract her learners.

Valencia begins a third list, noting pedagogical processes that she needs to modify in order to motivate her learners and engage them actively in their own learning. Instead of mass-producing worksheets, Valencia decides she will create her own handouts, and many fewer of them, by concentrating on projects that focus on cooperative learning and sharing outcomes with one another in class. Although Valencia is aware of the increased noise that may accompany her approaches, she is eager to transfer the responsibility for the learning to her students.

NE: Negotiate and 4
Evaluate Curriculum
and Content

W hen I tell teachers that every one of them practices censorship, they gasp in disbelief. But you do. You make an amazing number of decisions every day as to what to teach and what not to teach, how to teach and how not to teach, what and how to test, and what and how not to test. All of these activities constitute censorship.

Your decisions do not occur in a vacuum. You not only develop the curriculum, design the instruction, and select the assessments; you also decide who will receive specific information, access, and opportunities. For example, do you tell all of your students the same information or are some of the students out of hearing range, as in small groups or out of the classroom for many different reasons when you deliver instruction? Do you guide all of your students in accessing the same resources or do some students receive different guidance? And do you allow all of your students to participate equally or give all of them the same choices?

Teachers yield incredible power in their classrooms as they make their decisions regarding the curriculum and content. Just like becoming aware of your assumptions, values, and beliefs in Chapter 2, you probably are oblivious to the power of and responsibilities associated with your decision making from preparation to reflection. In this chapter, we move clockwise to the next point located on the Gallavan cultural competence compass, NE, and investigate how to "Negotiate and Evaluate the curriculum and content."

UNDERSTAND CURRICULAR DEVELOPMENT

Curriculum entails everything that happens in your classroom and around the school, including before, during, and afterschool hours involving teachers, students, parents, and the entire learning community (Oliva, 2004). Curriculum is not the list of subject standards and academic expectations that most teachers must know and follow. Curriculum incorporates all content, all processes, and all contexts of the entire educational environment. In addition, every educational environment includes a multitude of cultures.

Yes, you will be teaching specific content, such as language arts, math, science, social studies, music, art, physical education, foreign languages, and so forth, with key concepts and pertinent practices that members of the national professional learned societies have established as meaningful and relative to that subject at each grade level. For example, members of the National Council for the Social Studies have written and published ten themes of social studies that reach across the four primary subject areas of social studies; these include citizenship, economics, geography, and history. Collectively these four content subjects constitute the field of social studies. Every field of study includes several content subject areas.

The members of the respective national professional learned society have identified anticipated outcomes appropriate for students in each grade level that should be taught in Grade P–12 schools and classrooms within and across the primary subject areas. This curricular guide can be considered in terms of its scope, the items identified for a particular grade level and the sequence, and the flow of items from grade level to grade level. Teachers are responsible for helping their students learn all of the identified items at one grade level in preparation for students learning the identified items in the next grade level.

All content subjects connect to a national professional learned society whose members have written and published themes and standards. The members of national professional learned societies include classroom teachers, school administrators, university professors, and national experts. From these publications, members of state departments of education—again in collaboration with school administrators, classroom teachers, and university professors—have identified the state standards and academic expectations for each grade level so there is a specific scope with the grade level and a continuous sequence within the P–12 school system. As you can see, classroom teachers just like you serve on all curricular development levels.

The state standards and academic expectations also include specific outcomes related to teaching and learning. These outcomes guide the teacher's pedagogical strategies. Thus, combing the content standards, academic expectations, and pedagogical strategies establishes the foundation of the curriculum. Many teachers consider developing curriculum an enjoyable and rewarding responsibility. Drawing upon the requirements stipulated by their state, school districts, and schools, teachers create the artistry and self-expression of teaching through their curricular plans.

Integrating standards and expectations across their curriculum, teachers establish a sense of purpose to their unit and lesson plans.

During their curricular planning, teachers design strategies to (M) motivate their students; (I) implement the activities; (N) negotiate and nurture everyone's progress, and (D) determine the dispositions coordinated with the levels of proficiency cognitively, affectively, and socially. I call this approach MIND over matter (see Figure 4.1).

What *matters* are the degrees of success, satisfaction, significance, and sustainability that you include, and every student acquires, in your classroom. In other words, every student must experience achievement in the academics cognitively, physically, affectively, and socially. Achieving success and satisfaction in significant ways for both the student and the school will lead to sustainability for a student to continue individual

Figure 4.1 MIND over Matter

MIND			
M	I	N	D
Motivation	Implementation	Negotiation	Dispositions

Establishing and promoting reasons
 	
• to attend school,
• to complete the course or grade level, and
• to graduate from school.
	Guiding and guaranteeing that all students
	
	• feel safe and wanted,
	• engage and participate fully,
	• express learning and outcomes individually, and
	• are taught in developmentally appropriate ways.
		Modeling and reinforcing the practices of
		
		• cooperation,
		• compromise, and
		• connection,
		• empowering all students to have
		  ○ voice,
		  ○ choice, and
		  ○ ownership.
			Assessing and evaluating outcomes that are
			
			• cognitive
			• affective, and
			• social outcomes and attitudes related to
			  ○ advancement,
			  ○ interactions, and
			  ○ results.

Matter			
Success	Satisfaction	Significance	Sustainability
Achieving to the best of one's ability.	Finding personal pleasure and reward.	Comprehending the most important knowledge, skills, dispositions, and contexts with personal connections.	Continuing the procedures while in school and throughout life.

growth and development; with this sustainability, the student graduates from school and finds reward in life. Teachers must negotiate and evaluate the curriculum consistently and carefully to achieve success, satisfaction, significance, and sustainability for every student.

IDENTIFY CONTENT, PROCESSES, AND CONTEXT

Developing curriculum requires you to know your content, feature the standards, aim for the expectations, and anticipate outcomes that are developmentally appropriate for each subject area and grade level. For every student to achieve success, satisfaction, significance, and sustainability, the content must combine with the processes that all students must know and do in ways that meet the needs and interests of your particular classroom of students. This establishes the context. You can develop the finest curriculum in the world, but without context your curriculum has no purpose.

Let's walk through an example. You are assigned to teach third grade math, so you look at the state standards and academic expectations to identify what students need to learn and how students are expected to learn. What students need to learn defines the content; how students are expected to learn that particular content describes the processes. Some teachers can select their own textbooks and materials. For other teachers, the state, school district, or school may determine textbooks, teaching strategies, manipulatives, resources, and so forth.

However, each teacher is still responsible for combining these ingredients, writing a recipe, preparing a nutritious yet delicious meal, and serving the feast. The feast must be attractive, edible, and healthy for each diner. And, each diner has unique characteristics describing the diner's tastes, nutrition, digestion, experiences, and so forth. When planning a feast, you would consider that not every diner is the same. This analogy demonstrates the job of developing curriculum with important content and key processes set in the appropriate context of your classroom.

ALIGN CURRICULUM WITH INSTRUCTION AND ASSESSMENT

Once you equip yourself with the appropriate content, processes, and context, you must select the most effective teaching strategies and learning experiences. You want to match your teaching and your classroom activities with the curriculum. Now it is time for your curriculum to come to life.

Here is the key to your success: align the curriculum with your instruction and assessment so they fit together as one continuous event. There are three steps that will help you achieve this (Wiggins & McTighe, 2005).

1. Look at the content and processes. Categorize these items as:

   a. Big ideas that need to last a lifetime.
   b. Intermediate information that needs to be understood for now.
   c. Tiny details that need to be conquered immediately.

2. Look at the expectations. These are your endpoints. Sequence your content and processes beginning at the end and work backwards in four steps and address these questions:

   a. Assessment.

      i. How will you monitor progress and measure achievement?
      ii. What and how will you assess?
      iii. What and how will your students assess themselves?

   b. Instruction.

      i. How will you guide your students?
      ii. How will your students guide themselves?
      iii. How will your students guide one another?

   c. Curriculum.

      i. What is the scope?
      ii. What is the sequence?
      iii. What is the priority of the categorized content and processes?

   d. Purpose.

      i. Why are you using the curricular content that you have selected? Are the students connecting with the content?
      ii. Why are you using the instructional strategies that you have selected? Are the students engaged in the processes?
      iii. What are you using to align the assessment techniques with the curriculum and instruction? Are the students demonstrating achievement and recognizing their own progress?

3. Look at your students. To align your curriculum, instruction, and assessment, you have to place everything into a context. Consider these three questions and be thorough in your descriptions:

   a. What are the general characteristics of your class overall?
   b. What are the trends of the various groups of students in your class?
   c. What are the individual characteristics of each student?

Although you will constantly align your curriculum, instruction, and assessments throughout the school year, your attention should attune to the context of your class and students. You will make new discoveries every day—sometimes many times in a single day. The students are the reason you are their teacher.

RELATE TO INFORMATION, ACCESS, AND OPPORTUNITY

Your curriculum, instruction, and assessments must allow all students to gain the same information, attain the same access, and receive the same opportunities. This means that all students must be guided and supported in attaining full comprehension of the subject's content and interconnectivities of the content with the content of other subjects; extensive application of the content area's specific processes and associated resources; and equitable participation in all learning experiences.

Information, access, and opportunity do not occur for all students by all teachers in all classrooms and in all schools. Many teachers bring limited cultural competence with them into their classes and, by chance and by choice, do not ensure that all students receive the same information, access, and opportunity. You can develop the most wonderful curricular content, instructional strategies, and assessment techniques possible on paper; however, if you do not ensure equal information, access, and opportunity for all students, then you, too, have been a teacher who has not displayed cultural competence.

CONNECT WITH TEACHING, LEARNING, AND SCHOOLING

The fourth set of essential elements for negotiating and evaluating the curriculum and content require expanding your thinking even more (see Figure 4.2).

You and your classroom do not function in isolation. You and your classroom are part of the business of education with which you must be connected. Connection can be deconstructed into three components.

The first component comprises your teaching. You learned to teach from a variety of sources and more and more sources continue to influence your teaching. It is vital to continue your education through reading, university courses, and professional development. Subsequently, your teaching repertoire will expand and change over time. Ask any teacher whom you label one of the best and you will hear how that teacher has stayed current and enthusiastic over time.

Your teaching must fit with a school and school district. This means you must be aware of the changes in the students who come to school and especially their cultures and cultural characteristics. Your curriculum,

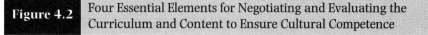

Figure 4.2	Four Essential Elements for Negotiating and Evaluating the Curriculum and Content to Ensure Cultural Competence

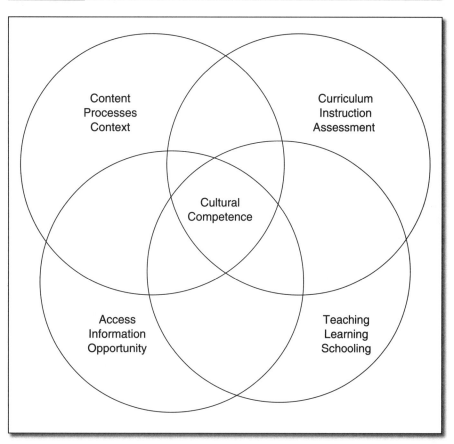

instruction, and assessments must be appropriate for every student to feel safe, be engaged, and experience achievement. Ask a colleague or an administrator to observe your classroom and review your plans, in other words, to mentor you with your cultural competence.

Likewise, your teaching must connect with the learning. After all, if students are not learning, then you need to review the efficacy of your teaching. Too many teachers tend to assign the responsibility of learning solely on their students and their families. Learning is your primary goal; use your critical thinking skills to analyze your strengths and weaknesses. Consider your classroom from the perspective of all your students as well as each one of your students. Would you be comfortable? Would you want to participate? Would you be inspired to produce? You may discover some harsh realities related to your cultural competence.

Teaching and learning dovetail with one another while placed in a context of schooling. Schooling occurs locally to globally; schooling entails the entire educational enterprise. The progress of your students will be reported through various mechanisms, such as standardized testing. Your classroom will be compared and contrasted to other classrooms—in your grade level, the school, the school district, the state, and even the United States. It is important to sharpen your focus, maintain your filters, and enhance the findings so you and your class function as effectively and efficiently as possible.

MAKE MEANING THROUGH SOCIAL CONSTRUCTIVISM

Developing the curriculum and connecting content to your students occur in multiple contexts. You bring your context; the students bring their individual and shared contexts; the school and society constitute a context. Through social constructivism (Vygotsky, 1978), your task is to make meaning of the learning for each player in this scenario.

Your curriculum, instruction, and assessments need to be developmentally appropriate in order for each student to understand the immediate information. This information provides the foundations for the continuing concepts that expand from grade level to grade level. As students construct their own meanings, they establish strong yet individualized foundations upon which unending understandings will build. The concepts and practices learned in Grade K–5 classrooms last a lifetime as students become adults and move through a variety of contexts.

TRANSFORM YOUR APPROACH AND CHECK YOURSELF

Ultimately, the goal is to transform your approach to teaching and learning as one emanating with and exemplifying cultural competence. Transformation may not happen easily or comfortably. After all, you are a product of your environment, and many teachers are limited in their education and life experiences.

The content and processes in your classroom must relate to every student and the relationships must occur in a context. This means that your teaching and learning must ensure that each student makes valuable and long-lasting connections to the content and processes, and that all students are guided and reinforced to learn about and understand all other students—locally to globally. These two aims constitute huge responsibilities for teachers and may seem nearly impossible for you to accomplish. First, you do not know each of your student's three levels of cultural characteristics in ways that will help each one connect with the content. Second, there does not seem to be enough time during class to make this happen, or time out of class for you to prepare. Third, getting each student to learn about and understand one another may seem impossible. Here are some suggestions to help you achieve this with ease and efficiency:

1. When you introduce a unit of learning or a lesson plan, ask your students to tell you what they already know and how they know what they know. These items constitute the first portion of a KWHL chart. You may need to dedicate an extra day to the unit to collect these data before you start. As you collect the K, or knowledge that students already know, ask questions of every student so you collect feedback from everyone. Make sure you also delve into how the students know the information or how the knowledge connects with the individual student. Using Socratic questioning to build in the moment and to include every student, you advance the learning and enhance participation immediately.

2. Record the collected data in words or drawings. You also can use icons as nonlinguistic representations.

3. As an alternate to recording the data, design your activity so the students contribute the data. Students can share what they know in small groups and report to the whole group. If you have non-readers and especially non-English readers, you could ask your parent volunteers to help record the data.

4. Establish your own comfort with sharing the exchange of knowledge, letting students take charge of their own learning and noise. If you feel challenged with these three conditions, you may need to transform your approaches.

5. While introducing new content and processes, allow plenty of time for students to ask questions and contribute their connections. You may experience some resistance, and wonder if you have the time. However, when you invite your students into the teaching and learning, you cover the material much more quickly and the material remains with the students much longer. Ultimately, time spent at the beginning of the unit frees your time and reduces your efforts to repeat and remediate later in the unit.

6. Ensure that all students participate in the classroom conversations and activities. To help regulate the students, employ your creativity. For example, a teacher I work with uses bright red plastic disks she found in a discarded board game. The teacher gives each student a disk, and the disk both restricts and requires students to talk one time. To begin, she places the students on competitive teams so the students reinforce one another to be successful.

7. Integrate multiple forms of expression throughout the unit in the forms of menus and rubrics. Rather than asking all students to create one identical product, offer your students the opportunity to create different products. This transformation will change every student (and you). Now the students are exposed to various ideas exponentially. Instead of hearing or seeing one or two ideas that you know or have the time to prepare, the students can "wow" one another with as many ideas as there are students. Again, you cover much more material in less time during the school year when everyone is both a teacher and a student.

8. Construct a bulletin board for the unit of learning for students to display their written work, drawings, and pictures conveying their connections to the unit. You will be amazed at the products that students either make or find to express their connections and from multiple perspectives.

9. Communicate with your students' families on the expectations accompanying your transformed approaches to teaching and learning. Once families comprehend that personal connections are not just accepted, but desired, families will contribute to the unit too.

10. Provide feedback and reinforcement frequently. In order to provide all of your students with equitable information, access, and opportunities, you must tell your students what you want and like in ways that your students accept and respect.

WATCH FOR BIASES AND HIDDEN AGENDAS

Since you are human and a product of your environment, most likely you possess some biases and communicate some hidden agendas. You may or may not even know the biases and agendas exist. Again, inviting a colleague to watch you and listen to you as you teach, and then provide you with honest feedback will help you the most. Be sure to ask a trusted colleague, and collaboratively establish the guidelines.

One major bias that many teachers possess relates to issues of fairness. Here are some questions to consider:

1. Where do you stand in your classroom when you teach?

2. Where is your desk located?

3. What students sit near where you teach and the location of your desk?

4. What is your path for walking around your classroom?

5. How much time do you spend with each student?

6. Is the time spent equitable for all students? Why or why not?

7. Are there any patterns associated with the students who sit near where you teach, where your desk is located, and where you walk around and stop most frequently and for longer periods of time?

8. Whom do you call on, for what kinds of questions or tasks, and how often?

9. What kinds of follow-up questions and feedback do you provide each student? Are the questions and feedback equitable and fair?

10. What types and amount of information, access, and opportunities do you provide each student, and why?

For the observation, provide your trusted colleague with a seating chart and ask the colleague to record your paths and the times you spend with students. You might be amazed and perhaps disappointed when your colleague reveals that you have biases. Take some time to analyze and reflect upon the feedback.

Some teachers have hidden agendas, and some of the agendas may not be as hidden as the teachers might believe. Some hidden agendas pertain to discrimination based on race, ethnicity, gender, social class, religion, size, language, and so forth. Again, asking a trusted colleague to provide exact transcripts of your words may enlighten you. For example, you may use a different tone with certain students; you may ask different levels of questions with certain students.

You may incorporate limited examples in the content and processes that convey a particular set of norms, such as: Families are composed of a mother and father. Everyone lives in a house. All students have parents (particularly fathers) who work. People go to work during the day and outside of the home. All families attend houses of worship and on Sundays. All families have parents who earned college degrees. Children in families who move frequently will be less successful in school. Large children are less intelligent and less motivated. The list of examples is endless.

Some teachers do not realize that they defer to unnecessary norms; these teachers both appreciate being enlightened and transform their teaching immediately, advancing their cultural competence. Unfortunately, some teachers are fully aware of their societal references. These teachers purposely maintain their unrealistic norms, denying their students an education that communicates cultural competence.

STRIVE FOR SOCIAL ACTION

As you plan and prepare your units of learning, start incorporating social action components. Keep them small and achievable. For example, if you are studying the community in social studies, discuss with your school administrator the possibility of inviting a specific speaker from a community agency that helps people in need. Talk with the guest speaker in advance of the visit so you are fully aware of the information that will be shared and any materials that will be distributed. Find out if the agency solicits any items that the students might be able to contribute. Before the guest speaker visits your classroom, tell your students' families that the guest speaker will be visiting and the reason for the talk; invite the adults in your students' families to join your class on that day.

After the speaker has left the classroom, initiate a conversation about ways people can help this agency. If it is appropriate, guide your students in organizing a social action project that donates items to this particular agency. Again, communicate your plans with your school administrator and students' families throughout the events. Integrate the social action project across the curriculum so students link the learning to literacy, math, science, social studies, and the fine arts.

The ideas for social action projects are unlimited. Also, not all of them require donated items that require students and their families to spend money. Examples include school and community clean-up projects, recycling projects, collecting items that people throw away such as soda-can tabs, making signs or materials for the school or another classroom, helping the school librarian and other school personnel, teaching other students, assisting the before- and afterschool care programs, and so forth.

KEEP CURRICULUM HONEST, NATURAL, HOLISTIC, AND AUTHENTIC

All approaches for transforming your curriculum to ensure cultural competence must be honest, natural, holistic, and authentic. Allow individual expression that is shared and respected with content and processes that cover a broad range of ideas and perspectives. These elements make it honest. Simultaneously, your curriculum, instruction, and assessments must align as one seamless event where students connect the learning to themselves and learn about all other students. These elements make it natural and holistic. Finally, cultural competence must be evident in the teaching, learning, and schooling so the context is authentic.

Cultural competence is an integral part of every learning experience—formal and informal. Start investigating and analyze your practices; set your sights on transforming your curriculum and content so they are honest, natural, holistic, and authentic for everyone.

DESIGN YOUR PLAN . . .

This chapter builds upon the imperative to start acting now in Chapter 1, the importance of setting your goals in Chapter 2, and the importance of noticing culture and cultural characteristics in Chapter 3. The next step is to begin designing your plan. You know the steps for developing curriculum to fulfill the state standards and academic expectations associated with specific content subject areas (Jacobs, 1997). Making your curriculum come alive in your context means negotiating and evaluating what you now realize should exist so every student can achieve success, satisfaction, and significance, and sustain these elements throughout school and life.

It will help to design a plan that allows success, satisfaction, and significance that will sustain you throughout your career. After all, teaching, learning, and schooling operate in unison so you are an intricate player in the game too. Start thinking about approaches you can adopt to ensure that you can decipher the items that are included and emphasized in the content, as well as the items that are absent or dismissed. It is essential to design a plan to assess what you need and want. Take inventory, allowing you to acknowledge what exists and identify what is missing. Then measure or determine the importance of each item, to consider ways to integrate items efficiently. Finally, organize and supplement the content and processes as you develop your curriculum so that all students can learn about themselves and one another in their own context (Huffman & Rickman, 2004).

Extending Activities for Teachers

1. Write the major cultural characteristics of groups and individuals representative in your classroom individually on index cards (i.e., Asian American, Black, Caucasian, Hispanic, Native American, female, male, wealthy, upper class, middle class, lower class, subpoverty- or poverty-stricken, Christian, Jewish, Muslim, English speaking, English language learning, etc.). Divide the cards into groups (i.e., race, ethnicity, gender, socioeconomic status, religion, language, etc.). You will discover that you do not know the cultural characteristics of some of your students and that some students' cultural characteristics are not distinct. You have students, maybe all of them, who are combinations of several cultural characteristics within one group. You will be amazed at the number of index cards that you fill. Next, look at the state standards and academic expectations identified for your subject area; think about the content that you plan to feature to fulfill the standards and expectations. Then, select one card and imagine that you possess that particular cultural characteristic. Is the cultural characteristic written on the index card visible in the curriculum and content? Place the cards to which you answer yes in one pile, and the cards to which you answer no in another pile. Your task is to find ways that every cultural characteristic represented in your classroom is visible in your curriculum and content.

2. If you are unsure if a student's cultural characteristics are visible in the curriculum and content, contact individuals and access resources for support. One place to begin is with your students' families. Send home a short questionnaire at the start of a particular unit of learning, giving a brief overview of the unit. List the state standards and academic expectations. Describe some of the activities that you intend to feature. Then ask a member of the family to reply to a section stating: "All students' cultural characteristics are valued and respected in our classroom. Please tell me one additional expectation or activity not listed here that I might add to our unit. Thank you." Family members may reply with an idea or they may call or e-mail you with more details. Some family members may even offer to visit your classroom to share their knowledge and expertise.

3. Visit the curriculum development office in your school district. Many school districts house resources for teachers to use to expand their curricula. The director of this office is also a valuable resource.

4. Check with your chamber of commerce to find a list of cultural centers in your community; then take a cultural excursion to learn more about the cultural characteristics of your students. Cultural excursions are much more comfortable and informational when you take a colleague with you, especially a colleague with whom you teach. You can help one another develop the curriculum and content for your classrooms.

5. Find resources on the Internet. Access authentic websites, representative of the various cultural characteristics. Resource C provides a list of websites to assist.

Extending Activities for Young Learners

Each of these activities should be modified for nonreaders, special education students, and English language learners as developmentally appropriate by using pictures instead of words, providing words for students to select instead of asking students to generate new words, listing possible vocabulary choices on the board, collaborating with learning assistants, and so forth.

1. When introducing a new unit of learning, use a KWL or KWHL chart to collect information from your students before you begin teaching. A KWL or KWHL chart is a large sheet of paper with the three or four letters written across the top or down the side. K stands for "know." Here you will record what your students already know. W stands for "want to know." Ask your students

what they want to learn related to the upcoming unit of learning. Collect information related to these first two letters prior to starting the unit to use as a guide. (There is no reason to use a KWL or KWHL chart if you do not intend to use the collected information to guide you.) Asking students what they want to learn provides you the keys to cultural competence. Ask some probing questions here so students will think critically and expand their feedback.

2. At the conclusion of the unit of learning, continue seeking feedback for the H and L. H stands for "how you learned." The processes of learning are equally important to the content of learning. You always want your students to be able to describe how they know or how they learned what they learned. The L stands for what was "learned." Now prompt your students to give you feedback not only associated with content and processes; ask about their connections with context and culture. This is your prime opportunity to evaluate your effectiveness in curriculum development.

3. Construct a graphic organizer such as the Venn diagram in Figure 4.2 to use when introducing a new unit of learning. Label the left side "expectation." Label the right side "outcomes." Guide the students in listing one expectation before starting the upcoming unit of learning. Expectations can include goals or objectives, or both. After the learning, return the graphic organizers and guide students in recording one outcome or something specific the student learned. Each student's outcome may be unique. Then, guide each student in identifying one cultural context connecting the expectation and outcome that serves as an example. For instance, if the expectation is "placing capital letters on proper nouns," one student's outcome may be "I learned that names of places need capital letters." In the center of the Venn diagram for the cultural context, the student will write one example, such "McGregor's Park." Then ask students to share all of their cultural contexts with the entire class orally or posted on a bulletin board to emphasize that the examples represent many different cultures.

4. When presenting new information in any content subject area, ask students to provide connections to their own lives by posing questions such as: "When you hear (or read) this information, what does it make you think about in your own life?" "When we study this information, what connections do you make to your home and family?" "These are big ideas or key concepts. What are some examples or some stories in your life that make the concepts real for you?"

5. While sharing a piece of literature, either fiction or nonfiction, ask students to give examples and stories from their own lives. You do not need to identify the examples as cultural contexts. However, as students share, continue to support and inform the entire class that examples in our individual lives exist in many different ways. Then model and reinforce by making cultural connections throughout the curriculum and content as the usual and accepted way of thinking.

Garrett has been teaching third grade at the same school for four years. He has been quite successful and was the recipient of the first-year teacher's award. Currently enrolled in a master's degree course on classroom management at the local university, Garrett has an assignment to write his professional biography introducing himself to his classmates with an assessment of some of his classroom management strengths and weaknesses. Here is his story.

I am a twenty-five-year-old, Black, African American man who is single, religious, and busy on weekends restoring my home that was my grandparent's home. I have been teaching third grade happily for four years; my mother was a teacher and I was not surprised when I decided to become a teacher. My mother predicted that I would teach high school English or drama, but during my first university observation in an elementary school classroom, I knew I wanted to dedicate my career to young learners. My life is much the same as my students' lives. Most of them are African American and living with their mothers with limited incomes. I grew up knowing only my mother. It seemed to me that we had enough money, but now I realize how my mother had to budget wisely so my siblings and I always had what we needed...and sometimes what we wanted. When I was ready to move out of my family home, I acquired my grandparent's home down the street since I wanted to stay in the neighborhood. Many of my students live with or near their grandparents too.

When I reflect on my first four years of teaching, I realize that my strengths feature transforming the classroom into a shared learning environment where every student has a sense of ownership. Most of my students own very little in their lives so it is easy for me to let them own the classroom. However, owning the classroom means they also have the responsibility for caring for the classroom. Caring for the classroom means caring for one another and themselves. This sense of responsibility is not one that most of my students experience in their daily lives so I have to introduce the concepts to them, model the practices, and reinforce their growth at every step.

I have never been afraid that I might lose control or be unable to regain control. I started small with some short student conversations and minor decision making. I reassured the students that our outcomes would impact only our classroom and for just one time. I used this experience to introduce the concept of our community. Then I incorporated more opportunities for shared decision making, allowing the students more voice and choice. I was impressed with the freedom that resonated throughout our community.

I wanted the students' families to become a part of our community. After all, I will be their teacher for only one year; the students are attached to their families forever. Families are eager to know that their children are safe, happy, and learning. All three concerns include physical violence and verbal abuse, such as bullying from other students, the teacher, and school administrators. In questionable situations, most family members believe that their children are right and that their children are recipients of various forms of hate stemming from all kinds of causes. I knew that families had to become active members of our community of learners too.

Throughout the school year, the students and I frequently invite family members into our classroom individually, as members of small groups, or as a whole group. My goal, centered on one of my weaknesses, is to bridge the beliefs that families fear teachers and schools or consider them the enemy, or that teachers and schools fear families or consider them the enemy. I want to transform the relationship to being conavigators in this journey. I want the families to realize that they can share all kinds of information and insights that will illuminate the path of cultural competence so home and school travel together.

E: Establish Community and Context

5

This chapter holds the most valuable keys to your success. Here you will discover the importance of "Establishing community and context"—E on the Gallavan cultural competence compass—creating a sense of place that invites, ignites, excites, and delights every student . . . and you. Nothing is more essential than getting your students (and yourself) to come to school eager to learn and share.

When adults reflect upon their own years as a student in school, rarely do their first thoughts race to a particular textbook or unit of learning. Most adults remember their classrooms, their friends, and their teachers. Memories about school resurrect thoughts and feelings about the people much more than the academics. Some of the memories are warm and wonderful; they bring smiles to our faces and we are eager to share our stories. Other memories are sad and scary; although suppressed, these memories continue to haunt us, shaping our attitudes and actions related to schooling, particularly for teachers.

If you want to be a teacher who is remembered positively, then you want to transform your classroom into a welcoming environment where your students feel safe and wanted (Hollins, 1996). Your students need to know that they will be respected at all times by all people. Your students need you as the teacher to care about them as people first and as students second.

CREATE A SENSE OF PLACE

Your first task may seem obvious, especially for most elementary school teachers in the primary grades. You are going to create a sense of place where the classroom focuses on the students and their learning. The space reflects who they are and what they are doing; it comes alive with their presence.

To create a sense of place, you need to increase your awareness to see and hear your classroom through the eyes and ears of your students (Leonard & Plotnikoff, 2000). To achieve this, get on your knees (to the best of your ability) and look around your classroom. Ask a colleague who is similar to you in size to pretend to be the teacher while you pretend to be a student. This brief exercise may be one of the most insightful experiences for you to initiate your awareness of the world in which your students live—a major aspect of cultural competency.

Kneel next to one of the chairs where your students will sit and ask your colleague to walk around the classroom and talk in the ways that most teachers teach. Can you see the teacher easily and hear the teacher clearly? Are there windows or displays that block your view or distract your attention? What about noise from either inside the classroom or outside the classroom?

As you project an image of yourself as a student in your own classroom, imagine that all of the other students are sitting in their chairs too. What are your thoughts and feelings about the space? Are you too close or too far away from other students? What are your thoughts and feelings about sharing the space with people you know such as your friends and people you don't know? What are your thoughts and feelings about sharing the space with people both like and not like you in gender, race, ethnicity, religion, language, socioeconomic status, and so forth?

Next, can you access all of the resources located in the classroom such as bookshelves, supplies, the water fountain, and the door? Would you feel comfortable walking to each of these resources without drawing unappreciated attention to yourself? Is the classroom arranged in rows, groups, or half circles? (See Figure 5.1.) How does the arrangement make you think and feel?

Finally, ask your colleague to move next to you at a student desk and act like the teacher helping you with an assignment. How close do you like the teacher to be to you? What do you see? What do you hear? And, maybe, what do you smell? What is your level of comfort? What does the teacher do that you like? What does the teacher do that you do not like? Consider your thoughts and feelings if the teacher is not your gender, your race, your ethnicity, religion, language, or your socioeconomic level. Would you notice? How would it affect you?

Figure 5.1 Classroom Configurations

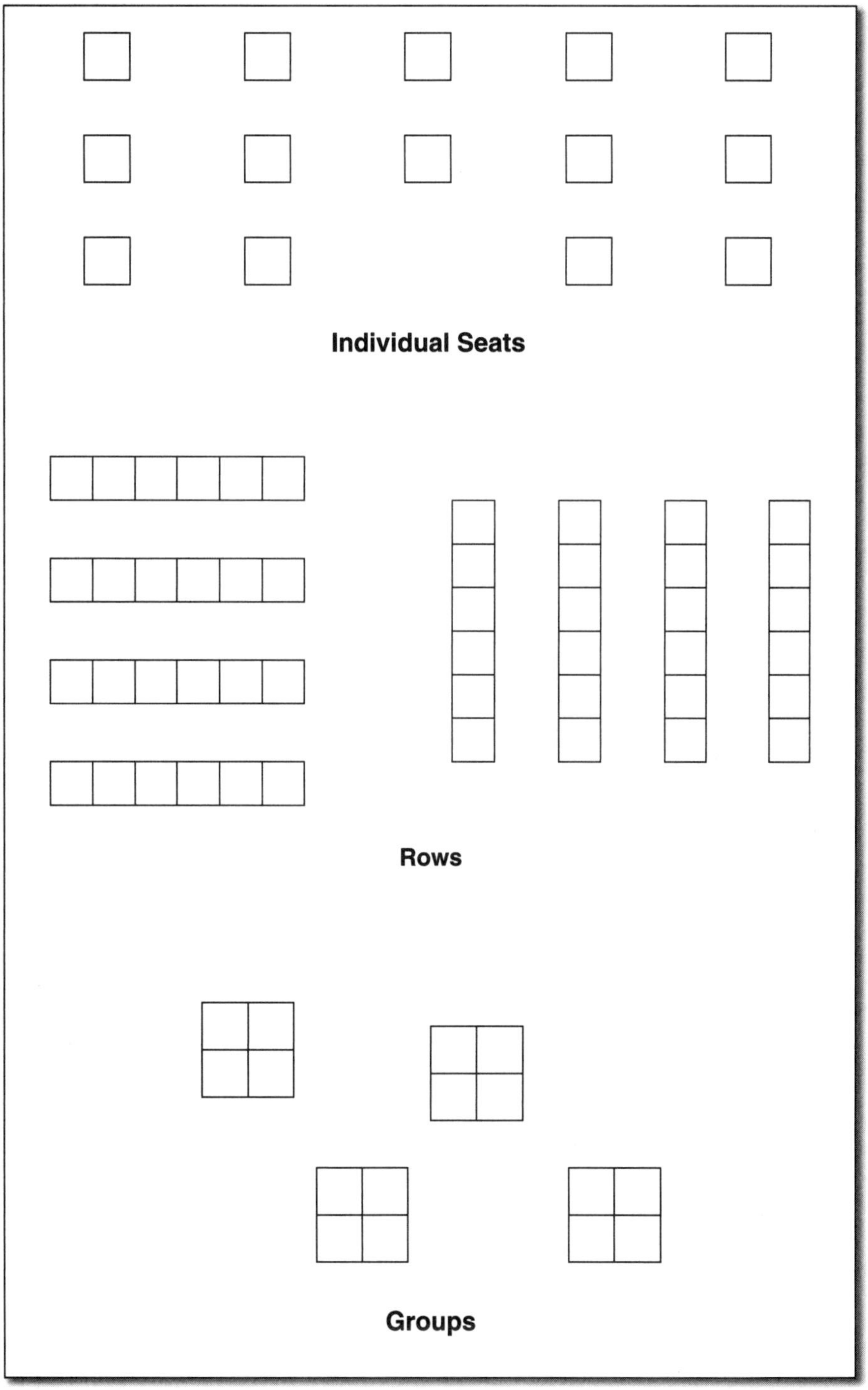

Individual Seats

Rows

Groups

(Continued)

(Continued)

Half Circles

INITIATE CULTURAL COMPETENCE FROM DAY ONE

There are five goals to fulfill in creating a sense of place; all manifest cultural competence and should be followed in this sequence. Additional guidelines for each item are provided in the following sections.

1. Make the classroom physically accessible. Before students and their families ever arrive, be sure everyone can find your classroom easily. Signs should be written clearly and posted in locations where people of all ages can read them. The signs may need arrows as well. Be sure your name and the grade level or subject area is posted on the classroom door.

2. Make the classroom socially welcoming. As students and their families approach your classroom, post signs and pictures that welcome them. If your classroom is known by a particular theme or mascot, you can post pictures of the theme or mascot outside the door. Your classroom should let people know that they are in the right place and that they will be comfortably accepted.

3. Make the classroom emotionally safe. The physical environment communicates your thoughts and beliefs about students and learning. Look at the wording on posters such as classroom expectations, bathroom and drinking fountain procedures, consequence charts, and so forth. Place your desk near the back of the classroom so people can visit with you privately. The back of your classroom may or may not be near the door so be sure

people entering the classroom can get to your desk quickly and easily. Smile as often as possible.

4. Make the classroom personally reflective. The classroom is a shared space, so the walls should have various bulletin boards where the students can display their products. Include bulletin boards for academic as well as artistic expressions.

5. Make the classroom mentally achievable. Notice that this last item is the only one in the list related to the academics. Although many people believe that schools are focused on academics, the academics can't happen until the students have arrived, and they feel welcomed, emotionally safe, and personally connected. Now the learning can begin. Everyone wants to find success in the classroom so the academics must be developed to be both challenging and rewarding, individually and for the group.

EMPHASIZE CLASSROOM APPEARANCE AND MOVEMENT

Students need to be able to enter a classroom and leave it easily; they leave at various times for various reasons, especially for individual needs that should be honored and respected. Some students will need to move around from time to time. Plus, everyone must be able to move around the room without tripping over furniture, cords, supplies, jackets, and backpacks. There must be clear paths all around the room; you and your students will have many different needs. Prepare your classroom accordingly before your students arrive on the first day.

Notice where you store books and materials and how you expect students to access these, both with and without your assistance. Consider if the items are located in logical places and if everyone can reach the items. If you want your students to develop a sense of responsibility, then make some items available to your students to access without you needing to manage them. This means trusting every student to honor and abide by the group's expectations. You must model and reinforce fairness for all students at all times. Some teachers may not trust all of their students based on the students' cultural characteristics. You need to assess your own beliefs.

ENSURE THAT THE CLASSROOM REFLECTS EVERYONE

As you select posters to hang on the walls, consider the messages on the posters, particularly the people in the pictures. Are the people shown in the pictures representative of not only the students in your classroom, but also all the students across the United States? You know that a picture's worth a thousand words. You want to capitalize upon every space in your classroom so your students identify with their learning community; the learning should be all about them. Additionally, dedicate a large bulletin board to display the students' products. Give each student a clip so the individuals can decide upon the specific products to share with their peers.

Allocate one bulletin board to the student of the week; you may have to feature two students per week depending on the number of students in your classroom. It is essential to not omit any students from participating in this activity. The students of the week bring personal photographs and items that can either be pinned to the board or placed on a table in front of the board for other people to see. The items can include toys, books, collections, and so forth. Then, dedicate time during the week for each student of the week to share the items with the entire class. Allow students to ask the student of the week questions; this approach helps students gain confidence and learn about one another.

To empower your students with resources, all students must be able to see and hear you and the various display areas at all times. Some students will not tell you that they cannot fully see or hear. The displays should be useful and also written so students can understand them. Be sure that students understand the various resources available in their classroom, and which resources are readily accessible for them, and which ones are reserved for the teacher.

Give your students permission to access as many resources as possible; the fewer times they have to interrupt you, the more time they will have to learn and you will have to teach. Plus, if the space is truly a shared community of learners, then students should be as independent as possible.

WELCOME AND GET TO KNOW YOUR STUDENTS

Stand at the door and say hello to every student and every family member as they enter the classroom. Use the words, "Welcome to *our* classroom. I'm so happy you are here with *us*." Notice the emphasis on the words *our* and *us*; you are starting to build a community of learners from the first meeting. Be sure that there is a desk and chair for each student and that there is furniture that fits each student. If you are writing students' names on their desks, coat hooks, cubbies, and so forth, wait until the students arrive on the first day of school so they can tell you the names they want you to use and exactly how to spell their names.

Likewise, let your students select the colors of items that you will be distributing. In addition, it is beneficial to allow students to choose where they want to sit on the first day of school. Be aware if you begin to guide students toward particular places based on their cultural characteristics. You can then move desks as necessary throughout the school year. Decorate only a few bulletin boards before your students arrive. Design activities to be completed during the first few days of school so your students write, draw, and construct products that are displayed. All of these approaches contribute significantly to making the classroom all about them.

Your students are excited about coming to school in two distinctively different ways. They are eager to be with their friends; that part is easy. But they are apprehensive to be with you. Primarily, they want to know if you will like them; that part makes them anxious. There are many stimuli to absorb during the first few days of school, and you have this one opportunity to create a safe sense of place through your words, actions, and interactions. Speak gently, be prepared with activities, and listen.

An emotionally safe classroom also means giving close attention to the types of displays you post in your classroom, the locations of the displays, and the wording not only on the displays but the words you use to describe the displays. For example, every teacher wants and needs to communicate what are commonly referred to as classroom "rules." Try using the words *expectations* or *etiquette*, rather than the word *rules*. You can explain the meaning to your students.

Instead of posting the classroom expectations that you project as necessary, schedule time during the first day of class to hold a class meeting or divide your class into small cooperative learning groups, and let the class develop the classroom expectations. You will be amazed at the results. Most likely, your students will design the same expectations that you planned to post, but through this type of activity, you have developed a community of learners. You can imagine the first words out of their mouths when they get home on the first day of school when describing their day: "We got to write our own classroom expectations."

Navigating cultural competence means taking time for developing relationships before attacking the tasks. Teaching, learning, and schooling constitute a three-pronged people business. One does not occur without the other two. Therefore, you must become acquainted with the players before you start to play.

You want to know your students both as people and as students. Perhaps you did not realize that these two labels are different. Think about yourself as a person. Think of your cultural characteristics describing your physical, mental, emotional, social, and personal qualities, as well as your abilities and choices. There is no other person quite like you.

When thinking about yourself as a student, cultural characteristics associated with you in an academic context apply. Your cultural characteristics describing your cognitive functioning, psychomotor skills, and your affective as well as psychosocial dispositions must be considered. Again, there is no other student quite like you.

There are many techniques for getting to know the people in your class as both people and students. Start with the people aspects, and then move to the student aspects. An individual who is less successful in an academic context may be quite successful in a personal context. Be careful not to let a weakness in one vein negate possibilities in the other vein. You want to give every student the chance to be known in every way.

HELP YOUR STUDENTS TO KNOW ONE ANOTHER

Concomitantly, you want to help your students to get to know one another. To create a learning community where everyone feels safe and welcomed, the community members must be guided in knowing, appreciating, and respecting one another. Two of the most important techniques that will empower students to listen to one another are (1) for you to stop talking and (2) for you to stop repeating what students say during class discussions.

It is challenging for teachers to stop talking. There is a false belief that when teachers talk, students learn. However, students learn much more when they are talking and when they are listening to one another. For example, during math, write the sample problem on the board. Instead of talking through the steps yourself, let one of the students do the teaching. You instantly empower the student who is teaching, and you inspire the other students. You must be cognizant of the student whom you select to do the teaching. Be sure that you select fairly throughout your teaching.

When students ask questions, ask other students to answer the questions. Again, you are empowering your students, assessing their progress, and increasing the learning. Students want to talk with one another, and they will get to know one another.

When students answer your questions, do not repeat their responses. Instead, build upon the first response by asking a follow-up question. Without echoing the first student, you force your students to listen to the discussion closely. Encourage your students to turn their chairs or desks so they are looking at one another and not you. Again, you want them to know, talk with, and listen to one another.

Helping your students to know one another also means incorporating personal connections to the curriculum and instruction frequently. Integrate questions so students provide their own examples from their own lives. Once you discover that your students are scouts, on teams, attend a particular afterschool program, and so forth, you can make those connections too. Be sure that you know something about all of your students and that you help guide your students to know something about all other students in the classroom. Unfortunately, some teachers overlook some students by chance and by choice based on the students' cultural characteristics. Again, you want to emphasize fairness and equity.

AVOID UNINTENDED CONSEQUENCES

It is challenging for some teachers to rethink setting up the classroom or interacting so the classroom is a shared environment honoring cultural competence. Reflect on the classrooms where you have been the student and try to recall techniques your teacher employed for you to feel welcomed and to know the other students. Perhaps no images come to mind.

Now reflect on the classrooms where you have been the teacher or watched the teacher. Identify any techniques that the teacher used to establish community so all students were acquainted and comfortable with one another. Again, no or few images may arise.

Most likely, the role modeling from your childhood past and your immediate past is limited or nonexistent, emphasizing the importance for you to establish specific goals and itemize your procedures to create a safe and welcoming learning environment where everyone knows one another and achieves to the best of each student's abilities. To avoid unintended consequences (Merton, 1936) that you never meant to create and had not anticipated, here are some steps:

1. Design at least six different ways to arrange the students' desks and chairs so you are ready to change the learning environment. Be sure all students can move around the room easily and see everything without obstructions.

2. In your designs, place the students in various groups so they get to know one another.

3. Check your plans so that students sit in various parts of the classroom, which includes near and away from the teacher's desk or other group settings around the classroom.

4. Consider various points where you can stand and sit to teach, and vary your placement.

5. Map the path you follow when you teach and when you assist students. Be sure that you are near all students equally.

6. Notice the amount of time you spend with each student so you are fair.

7. Listen to the types of questions you ask each student and the types of statements you provide as feedback and follow-up. Again, note equity and fairness.

8. Identify the kinds of connections you help students make to their own individual worlds to personalize the learning. Try and link at least one part of the curriculum to each student's life outside of school. If you cannot connect to each student, then you need to adjust your strategies right away.

CONNECT FAIRNESS WITH LEARNING

All students in Grades K–5, at some point in their life experiences, have not only sensed that they were not being treated fairly, but they have seen events and heard exchanges among other students as well as adults that did not seem fair. Young students feel safer and more comfortable announcing that something they have experienced or witnessed may not seem fair; older students tend to be cautious and more reserved. Everyone stores the events away in their brains as they continue to understand the people and world around them.

Students are not the only ones who have thought or expressed, *that's not fair,* through their words or body language. Most adults have experienced or witnessed situations that they consider to be unfair for themselves and for other people, especially parents and families observing their children's experiences in classrooms and schools. Like their children, some parents and families feel safer and more comfortable; these parents and families will contact the teacher or principal to question the situation and learn the whole story.

Some parents and families tend to be cautious and more reserved; these parents and families may not contact the principal or teacher. These parents and families may ignore the situation or find their own solution. The solutions may result in positive or negative outcomes for the student and teacher. From all situations, both the students and the adults will learn more lessons about social interactions that will affect them throughout their lives.

Many students do not like school because they sense that the educational environment is not fair. Students often report that learning is not tailored to their individual needs and interests, and they therefore are not invested in the learning process, especially lectures and testing. Students frequently see little purpose in school and that usually leads to boredom;

many students feel a lack of respect at school (from students and adults) and they feel little or no ownership in their own learning.

Not only does the educational environment seem unfair, but the students along with their parents and families feel there is little or nothing they can do about it. This sense of hopelessness can overwhelm a student's ability to function and learn. When hopelessness begins in Grades K–5, young learners establish a solid path toward dropping out of school as soon as possible. Dropping out of school is accompanied by an abundance of conditions that reduce a person's chances of success throughout life as well as the person's ability to parent effectively, thus influencing future generations.

When some students in Grades K–5 begin their path toward dropping out of school, they start causing additional challenges for their schools, classrooms, communities, and friends. The student withdraws mentally and emotionally from classroom interactions. Some educational researchers have relabeled this phenomenon as being pushed out of school. And, sadly, being pushed out of school may be caused by classroom teachers and school administrators through their lack of cultural competence.

Fairness has many facets. Imagine a large crystal with many different sides or faces. If you try to look through the crystal, the view is distorted. If you hang the crystal in a window, light refracts through the prism, projecting a rainbow across the room. Yet we use the word *crystal* to describe clarity; we say that an idea or outcome is "crystal clear."

A crystal is like the many facets of fairness. What one person thinks is fair may not match what another thinks is fair. People may be in complete opposition to one another in their definitions of fairness or, more likely, they may partially agree and disagree. Fairness is not a concept that means the same thing for every person.

Your responsibility emphasizes establishing a community of learners based on cultural competence where students sense fairness in the content and processes, that is, what they are being taught, how they are expected to learn, and ways they are allowed to express their learning. This means the curriculum must be personalized so the outcomes relate to their future learning and lives.

FEATURE CLASSROOM MEETINGS

Students will achieve much more in their classroom academically and socially if you conduct classroom meetings regularly. A classroom meeting involves establishing a series of days and times when students can talk with you and one another about school. Think of it like your family meetings. This is an opportunity to step back and allow your students to have an authentic voice in their classroom by talking about this place where they spend most of their time and energy. During classroom meetings, you can also orchestrate opportunities for them to vote or select outcomes. This process is called giving students choice.

When an individual has both voice and choice, the individual develops a sense of ownership. Ownership transforms individuals so they take care of themselves and the world around them. Ownership also increases respect and regard for other people that extends across society. Think about times that you were allowed to say what you wanted to say, and select what you wanted to do. Soon you viewed that situation as yours, giving you ownership resulting in enhanced care. Here are steps for conducting a classroom meeting:

1. Set the date and time; do not change the date and time without a worthy cause, accompanied with extensive explanation and negotiation with the students.

2. Direct students to put away all books, papers, and any other distractions so everyone is focused and can participate in the classroom meeting.

3. Run the classroom meeting in a professional manner.

4. Lead the meeting yourself, or once students understand the process, allow students to lead the meeting.

5. Write the agenda on the board. Ask students to contribute agenda items both in advance of the meeting and at the start of the meeting.

6. Prioritize the agenda items so they are presented logically and the meeting is conducted within the allocated time.

7. Present each agenda item as a discussion, not an announcement. For example, "The principal wants our class to start walking to the lunchroom using Hall A instead of Hall B. Let's talk about this request and what it means for us." Then allow students who want to talk and students who want to ask questions to engage in the conversation. Guide the conversation so students identify the choices and, in the case of the example, understand the principal's perspective. Even if the item is non-negotiable, students will take ownership, show pride, and comply with a request more readily once they are given voice, choice, and ownership.

8. Stay on task and watch the time closely. Students may view classroom meetings as the chance to redirect the teacher and avoid schoolwork. You are still in charge.

9. Be fair and expect all students to be fair. Classroom meetings involve democratic principles that require students to listen, make decisions, and express their thoughts. Ensure that everyone who wants to speak is afforded an opportunity to speak. You may need to establish systems allowing students to speak one time and within a limited amount of time.

10. Maintain civility that honors and respects cultural competence. If students express various perspectives, they must demonstrate respect for one another. Be aware that some individuals and groups may attempt to dominate the classroom meeting.

11. Write a word or two next to items on the agenda so students know the outcomes, next steps, and expectations.

12. Decide the date and time of the next classroom meeting. You can post a draft of the next agenda where students can add items between meetings. Guide students through the appropriate procedures for contributing agenda items.

BECOME A REFLECTIVE DECISION MAKER

Similar to wanting your students to participate in classroom meetings to become reflective, it is also vital that you become reflective in your cultural competence. Your cultural competence involves personal growth and professional development toward pedagogical expertise. It is a never-ending journey.

As you establish community and context based on cultural competence, you encourage your students to attend school and arrive to class on time while motivating them to participate and do their best; you also communicate the foundations of success for their future learning, family dynamics, and lifelong work worlds. These are the lessons that seem to resonate with learners far longer than the curriculum and instruction.

To ensure that you are becoming culturally competent, using it in your classroom, and teaching it to your students, take time to reflect upon your practices. Ask yourself three important questions:

1. Does this classroom welcome everyone equally in every way? This question addresses the community.

2. Is the learning understandable, personalized, and achievable? This question addresses the context.

3. Am I fair to each student, respectful of each student, and helping all students to learn about themselves and one another? This question addresses the cultural competence.

SHARE THE SPACE . . .

It cannot be emphasized strongly enough that the classroom is a shared space. If you refer to it as "my" classroom, students will always feel like guests. If you are not practicing cultural competence, the guests will feel unwanted. It is doubtful that many teachers try to achieve these outcomes; yet, such small steps will change the entire journey. The journey isn't really yours; you are the cartographer and navigator. You want your students to become both the drivers of their own learning and lives, and the passengers riding with other drivers.

Extending Activities for Teachers

1. Think about the range of experiences throughout your life as a member of a group, especially in schools and classrooms. What elements of the group made you feel safe and welcome? What activities did you like? Conversely, what elements of the group made you feel uncomfortable and, perhaps, unwanted? What activities seemed to leave you out? Once you have explored and identified elements that made the group experience more attractive and more rewarding as well as the elements that made the group experience less inviting and less enjoyable, you can begin to plan approaches that will help you establish a community and context that features cultural competence.

2. Talk with your professional colleagues about approaches that work in their classrooms for establishing communities and contexts. All teachers have tried a variety of approaches and will gladly share what has worked and what has not worked for them. If you can, take time to visit other teachers' classrooms to see their environments. Perhaps some colleagues use classroom meetings and you could watch the meetings take place.

3. Search the Internet for ideas and suggestions. There are many different ways to establish community and context; most websites offering guidance for teachers include strategies. Resource C provides a list of websites you can add to your search.

4. Invite students' families into your classroom to talk about their cultural characteristics. Young students greatly enjoy their family members visiting their classrooms and talking about their families, and most families are eager to share. Be sure to send a list of guidelines to the individuals who are planning to share. Guidelines should include the amount of time allocated for sharing, typical topics

that families tend to share with your particular grade level, if artifacts can be passed around and touched, if food can be included when sharing, and so forth. You also need to guide your guests with logistics such as locating a place to park, checking in at the main office, or bringing other family members or animals to your classroom. Your school administrators and colleagues can provide specific expectations pertaining to your school.

5. Likewise, invite various community members to visit your classroom and share their background and expertise. There are many people in communities who want to be a part of the school, yet they have no children enrolled in that particular school. Community members may be associated with a particular group or agency. Again, be sure to share guidelines for visiting classrooms with your guest speakers.

Extending Activities for Young Learners

Each of these activities should be modified for nonreaders, special education students, and English language learners as developmentally appropriate by using pictures instead of words, providing words for students to select instead of asking students to generate new words, listing possible vocabulary choices on the board, collaborating with learning assistants, and so forth.

1. Ask students to draw a picture of their favorite classrooms and to share their drawings with other students in a small group. Sit with each group as the students share their pictures. You can sit with each group if the other groups are given a second assignment to complete at the same time. Then rotate through the entire class to hear each description.

2. Each week, assign one student to assist any new students who enter the classroom. Most classrooms have new students who appreciate having another student assigned to help them know their way around the school, the locations of materials and supplies, and the regular routines in a classroom. An alternative approach is to assign one or two students to serve as the teaching assistants. These students answer other students' questions and address their concerns at the teacher's direction.

3. Create a place in the classroom where one or two students are featured each week. Encourage the featured students to bring family photographs and personal items to display such as their favorite books, sports memorabilia, and other special items. The featured

students should be provided a time to tell the other students about their displays. If you have two featured students in one week, invite students to share on a different day so each student has a special day of their own.

4. Organize a bulletin board related to the curriculum where students can post their own work. Include academic and artistic expressions so all students can see and appreciate one another's products.

5. Establish a rotating roster of classroom leaders so each student serves as a leader for two or three weeks. Determine in advance the role and responsibilities of each leader; then be sure to allow the classroom leaders to fulfill their responsibilities. Classroom leaders should be appointed not elected, avoiding the appearance of popularity contests.

Stacy is a White, European American, middle-class, religious, married woman who has been teaching kindergarten for twelve years. She was divorced with one child earlier in her teaching career, and now she is married with two additional children. She has taught in two different school districts and three different schools; her moves have been related to changes in her personal life so she could be closer to her family.

During high school and college, Stacy traveled extensively throughout the United States and around the world. Her father and mother are university professors and along with Stacy's sister Whitney, they all enjoyed touring during their academic breaks.

During her years of teaching kindergarten in various locations, Stacy has interacted with many different student populations. She is extremely comfortable around all cultures and welcomes all students and their families into her classroom. Students connect with Stacy as their teacher quickly and enjoy learning from her.

However, during those years, Stacy also has encountered resistance among some of the students' families as well as her colleagues. Some of the families' comments stem from Stacy's efforts to ensure that all students interact with all other students and that all students are afforded equal access and opportunities. Stacy recognizes that families want everything they can for their own children; families want to protect their children from any possible harm or pain. Stacy knows these sensations well, having moved several times to accommodate her own children's lives.

However, Stacy has learned that occasionally, families may expect unreasonable outcomes that do not reflect cultural competence. At these times, Stacy has been asked to offer one set of opportunities and to use one set of expectations for some students that are not offered or used with other students. These seemingly prejudicial requests tend to fall along socioeconomic lines that may match the race, ethnicity, gender, and family structure of particular students.

Over the years, Stacy's colleagues and even her administrators have expressed similar opportunities and expectations. Stacy acknowledges that individuals' resistance to cultural competence center on control and power. Although this appears to be an easy answer, it is accompanied by a complicated situation that is both difficult to stop and challenging to reroute. Individuals with control and power do not want to release them.

Stacy has seen that people who enjoy having control and power tend to reap both external and internal rewards. She has noticed her fear of not pleasing individuals with control and power increases the individuals' control and power, so her solution is to remove herself as best she can from the situation or confrontation and continue on her path. Regardless of the discomfort she tries to be herself and model the positive outcomes that her words and actions produce.

Stacy's goal is to maintain equity and respect for everyone. Rather than starting a discussion or confronting a family member or academic colleague when she realizes individuals possess different viewpoints, she focuses on the immediate tasks and work as collaboratively as possible. Stacy tries to avoid topics and issues that seem more contentious.

However, there have been occasions that Stacy has observed colleagues behaving with prejudice with students or other colleagues, so she has talked with her immediate supervisor or the assigned individual who is responsible for these types of concerns (department chair, school administrator, human resource personnel, and so forth). Usually, she receives insightful guidance and strong support so she can continue in her cultural competence.

SE: Seek and Engage in Collaboration and Construction

6

The responsibilities of teaching, learning, and schooling involve many different people. Although teachers may feel like they operate in isolation, no teacher acts alone. Teaching is based on the successes documented by past and present teachers and their effective strategies; likewise, learning is grounded on past and continuous theory and research. Teaching does not occur without learners, and learning does not occur without teachers. Both teaching and learning occur in the context of schooling. All three aspects should function optimally, and, most important, the teacher should not be the one doing all the work.

Therefore, you are strongly encouraged to seek and engage in collaborative exchanges with the multitude of individuals and resources all around you (Cushner, 2005). As educators, most teachers will generously share their ideas with you; they want their peers to be aware of their creativity and effectiveness. Similarly, most people outside of schools will also share with you once you tell them you are a classroom teacher. People in the community, near and far, generally have the deeply held desire to contribute to education. You simply need to explain your situation and ask for assistance (or materials) within reason.

Concomitantly, you want to engage in construction of new approaches and techniques, especially among your peers. Keep in mind that while you are seeking collaboration, so are your colleagues. Together, you and your colleagues can divide and conquer many different tasks by pooling your time, resources, and energy. This chapter, SE on the Gallavan cultural competence compass, provides you with specific guidelines that help you "Seek and Engage in collaboration and construction," building upon the foundations of your cultural competence found in earlier chapters.

NETWORK WITH COLLEAGUES

You will quickly realize that your job involves working with colleagues as much as it does working with your students. You rely upon your colleagues for every part of your success. You need them to tell you about the background and culture of the school, how it operates, whom to ask for various supplies and materials, where to go for forms, how decisions are made, and so forth. Schools are just like all other businesses and industries. Teachers are middle managers responsible for a group of workers, aka the students. All middle managers must work together cooperatively for the entire business, aka the school, to operate smoothly.

You not only need to assess your interpersonal social skills and interact effectively with your colleagues, but you need to be fully aware of your cultural competence. Teachers are people, too, representative of all cultural characteristics. You may want to revisit the list of foundations in Chapter 1, recognizing that differences must be valued and respected at all times and with all people.

Although the vast majority of teachers are White, European American, female, and middle class, teachers represent all races, ethnicities, genders, social economic classes, religions, languages, nationalities, geographic locations, family configurations, sexual orientations, political alignments, hobbies, and habits. As with all groups, the categories of cultural characteristics describing teachers are endless. However, many new teachers may falsely believe that all teachers are alike, simply because they are all teachers.

It is important to get to know all of your colleagues professionally and personally. They are both your coworkers and your friends. Teachers serve on many committees within their grade levels and subject areas as well as committees where they make decisions that impact whole school operations. To understand your colleagues' viewpoints and agendas, you must become acquainted with them. Most likely, you will encounter individuals with as many different sets of cultural characteristics and unique outlooks as there are individuals in your school. The faculty and staff at any school are (and should be) quite diverse.

Your colleagues will bring a wide range of dispositions related to teaching, learning, and schooling as well as the students, their students, and the immediate community that your school services. Again, you are urged to get to know your colleagues, but do not be surprised or caught off guard if your colleagues do not possess the same thoughts and beliefs that you have developed. Remember, faculty and staff are people too; you may discover that some of them are not as advanced with their cultural competence as you might have presumed or hoped.

You not only will be collaborating with your colleagues on schoolwide projects, you will be socializing with them too. You share office or planning-room spaces; you join various groups for lunch in the faculty lounge, offices, or classroom. Various groups of teachers form partially due to the time and location and partially due to personal choice. You may or may not be able to select the group or individuals with whom you will spend most of your out-of-classroom time.

Like all other businesses, schools involve individuals who serve in a variety of capacities. Most administrators and some teachers have earned advanced university degrees. Perhaps they use the title of "Dr." Classroom teachers and educational specialists also bring a wide variety of educational degrees and experiences. The school includes teaching assistants, clerical support, custodians, lunchroom workers, and playground supervisors. The staff members at any one school are just as diverse as the U.S. population; everyone should be valued, honored, and respected. You must be aware of your presumptions about all the individuals with whom you work.

Schools also operate with some individuals responsible for other individuals. Both official and unofficial protocols accompany hierarchies, and these protocols are all associated with power. Power is a significant component of cultural competence. Historically, selected cultural characteristics were automatically given power over other cultural characteristics. Some schools continue to operate within these presumptions in ways that are both overt and covert.

If and when individuals with power demonstrate control based on cultural characteristics, the situation is both uncomfortable and illegal. Recipients of the culturally based control have three choices: (1) they can address the concern directly and professionally if the individuals feel safe physically and for their jobs; (2) they can contact individuals in the offices of human resources where the individuals may or may not be supported; or (3) they can do nothing at all, hoping the situation will go away and not return. Throughout time, many people have chosen the third option in order to cope with the current situation the best way possible and to keep their jobs. Whether this solution is right or wrong, you must make wise decisions for your individual situation.

Schools tend to organize mechanisms for socializing across grade levels, subject areas, and job responsibilities. Administrators want everyone to interact cooperatively and supportively with one another. Your school may create a social committee, play secret pals, and hold holiday parties. You must conduct yourself professionally and with cultural competence in all academic and social settings on campus and in the community.

REALIZE THE POWER OF THE PROPINQUITY EFFECT

The propinquity effect states that there is a tendency that the more we interact with an individual, the more likely we are to become friends with that individual (Festinger, Schachter, & Back, 1950). Think about this situation. Most of us can remember becoming acquainted with an individual because we sat next to one another in a class, on an airplane, at a special event, and so forth. There was probably little or no chance that we would have gotten to know one another for any other reason, and yet, a friendship occurred due to the proximity.

The propinquity effect helps make classrooms and schools function well, but effectiveness requires insightful leaders who ensure that people are given time to get to know one another and that they are given a task that forces them to collaborate. When you work on a particular team at your school, you will need to collaborate with these individuals for your and your students' success. Initially, you may believe that you do not have much in common with these individuals or you have been led to believe that you will not like them. However, once you begin working together, you may discover that both prior beliefs were inaccurate. These same conditions and outcomes can occur in your classroom too.

VISIT OTHER TEACHERS' CLASSROOMS

One of the best ways to expand your cultural competence repertoire is to observe other teachers' classrooms while they are in action both in your school and at other schools. Contact the teacher whom you would like to observe in person or by e-mail; then meet with the teacher well in advance of the observation to talk about your purpose for the observation. Some of your colleagues may be uncomfortable with your being in their classrooms. Other colleagues will welcome you joyously; again, most teachers can't wait to share with a peer. These teachers love having another adult in the classroom to see them doing the things they do all the time.

Identify your purposes clearly and specifically with the teacher you plan to observe. Also, be open to the other teacher's suggestions. For example, if you want to look at the teacher's classroom organization and bulletin boards, you could arrange for a tour before or after school. These times would allow you to talk freely with the teacher so you can ask questions and record notes as you are visiting. This same approach applies if you want to look at the teacher's curricular design or resource materials.

You might be more interested in observing the teacher interact with students during specific times of the day. This establishes a different purpose. If you want to watch how the teacher opens the day, conducts a classroom meeting, or teaches a particular lesson, you will have to coordinate the time. Hopefully you have a planning time each day, or at some time during the week, while other teachers facilitate their classroom instruction when you could visit to observe. When you observe, be sure to seek permission from your administrator or department chair for your plans well in advance of the observation and wait for a reply.

The teacher in the observed classroom should introduce you to the students and explain that you are there to watch the teacher and gain some new ideas. The students will be impressed that teachers learn from one another just as teachers tell their students to learn from one another. Here is a list of items to observe during your visit. Consider each item in terms of respect for and equity among all cultural characteristics of all students.

1. Classroom seating arrangement.

2. Classroom displays infusing cultural competence.

3. Classroom warmth, safety, and comfort.

4. Student information regarding bathrooms and drinking fountains.

5. Teacher's formal interactions.

6. Teacher's delivery and directions.

7. Teacher's informal interactions.

8. Teacher's selection of students to answer questions, participate in activities, ask questions, serve as leaders, and so forth.

9. Student involvement in activities.

10. Student choice.

11. Student expression of outcomes.

12. Teacher's wait time.

13. Teacher's reactions, physically and emotionally.

14. Teacher's feedback statements and questions.

15. Teacher's techniques for probing and delving techniques.

16. Teacher's placement and movement during instruction.

17. Teacher's placement and movement during guided practice.

18. Placement of and access to teacher's desk.

19. Placement of and access to students' possessions.

20. Classroom behavior expectations (i.e., wording, placement of chart, consequences).

21. Classroom reward system.

22. Student displays.

23. Teacher's system for redirecting student energies.

24. Teacher's system for diffusing student energies.

25. Teacher's system for positively reinforcing student energies.

After the observation, tell the teacher you observe what you saw, heard, thought, and felt. Like you, the observed teacher will be anxious for feedback and new ideas. Stay positive and productive; your observation could expand to additional observations and even an exchange of observations. Most school administrators are ecstatic to hear that teachers have initiated in-school observations as professional development.

Keep in mind that you do not need to become exactly like the observed teacher. You will observe approaches and techniques that may or may not apply to you and your classroom. Likewise, you may observe interactions that you think are inappropriate and not culturally competent. You are not the supervisor; it is not your duty to report your observations. Nor should you share your observations with your colleagues. Draw wisely from the observation for your own self-reflection and cultural competence.

FIND A PARTNER AND A MENTOR

Two of the most rewarding steps to take in your teaching career are to establish a partnership and to locate a mentor. You may believe that these two roles can be shared by one individual; they should be two separate people, as you will be involved in very different activities with each of them and glean different types of professional growth.

Frequently, the teaching partner is another teacher in your same grade level and subject area so you can develop curriculum, design instruction, and align assessments together. Partners in the same grade level and subject area can also divide responsibilities for collecting resources and constructing products to use with students.

If you establish a partnership, be aware if you have left out a member or members of the grade level or subject area. Perhaps you project that it would be more expedient with only two teachers working together. However, there may be third or fourth members of the team who would like to work with you and it would be a logical combination. You may have included some teachers and excluded other teachers based on cultural characteristics—be aware of your actions at all times. All possible partners offer diverse ideas and insights associated with their cultural characteristics. It is wise to tap these resources for your teaching, your students' learning, and the success of the schooling.

You also want to locate a mentor. The administration may assign mentors, especially for novice teachers. Your mentor does not have to become your partner or a favorite friend. Your mentor helps you professionally so you demonstrate appropriate growth and development. You can ask your mentor the questions you need answered for you to understand the system and to advance your career. You must dedicate time and energy to your mentor, especially if the individual seems to operate within a different set of beliefs and expectations. You will benefit greatly by acknowledging the similar and different cultural characteristics independently, and then capitalizing upon the opportunities to stretch and grow (McCann & Johannessen, 2008).

EXPAND YOUR RESOURCES

Most teachers begin their careers with the basic materials to initiate their curriculum, instruction, assessment, and classroom management. From there, it is important to add more materials every year you teach. Some schools will provide materials or funding, or both, to purchase materials; other schools make no provisions and your acquisitions are your choice.

Since time, money, and energy are limited, make your choices powerful and as inexpensive as possible. You might have a curriculum resource library, either within your school district or at the local university in the teacher education department. These libraries will have materials that you can check out so you can copy the ideas that you want rather than purchase an entire book that may offer only a few pages that help you. The libraries may have some free or inexpensive resources available to purchase, or equipment to use to make your own materials.

Look in the telephone book yellow pages and on the Internet for various government and community agencies that might have materials to give you. You can acquire classroom sets of maps from the highway department and other state-related materials from the chamber of commerce. Individuals at the chamber of commerce can direct you to local businesses and industries that support classroom teachers. The immediate resources are endless.

The Internet offers unlimited resources as well. Resource C provides an extensive list of websites. One Internet resource can easily lead to another resource; your quest is to find the materials that match your purpose. Likewise, your partner, mentor, and other colleagues have conducted searches to expand their resources. Most of them will be glad to share.

The resources you bring into your classroom should support cultural competence. This means you should look at the materials to see that the photographs represent all of the United States, and in ways that communicate equity among all people, even if you consider the materials to represent your niche of the world. Remember, you are teaching all students about all other students.

Likewise, the materials should communicate cultural competence in the text. Watch for gender-neutral wording and any phrasing that may communicate discrimination. Also, be aware that a group with a public agenda sponsors the materials. Although the materials appear to extend your curriculum and they are free, avoid materials sponsored by private groups and companies.

INFUSE CULTURAL COMPETENCE

Think about cultural competence as a required academic subject area that you want to teach. For all academic subject areas, you consider the content and all the standards that the state has identified that students should know. The standards also include some processes that students should do. Then you place the content and processes in a context, identifying what students should be as respectful humans. This same pattern can be followed for cultural competence (see Figure 6.1).

As you construct the plans for your classroom, it is essential to infuse cultural competence everywhere all the time. At first, this approach may require you to plan within a specific frame that you develop based on your education, experience, and interactions with colleagues. A list of questions to ask yourself as you cross-check your plans includes the following:

1. Do the textbooks show pictures that represent all people, and all people equitably?

2. Do the pictures communicate the context in an unbiased manner?

3. Do the texts communicate the desired content?

4. Does the content of the texts infuse equitable representation of all people?

5. Is the language in the texts gender neutral and culturally respectful?

6. Do supplementary materials communicate the content and context equitably?

Figure 6.1   Cultural Competence Knowledge, Skills, and Dispositions

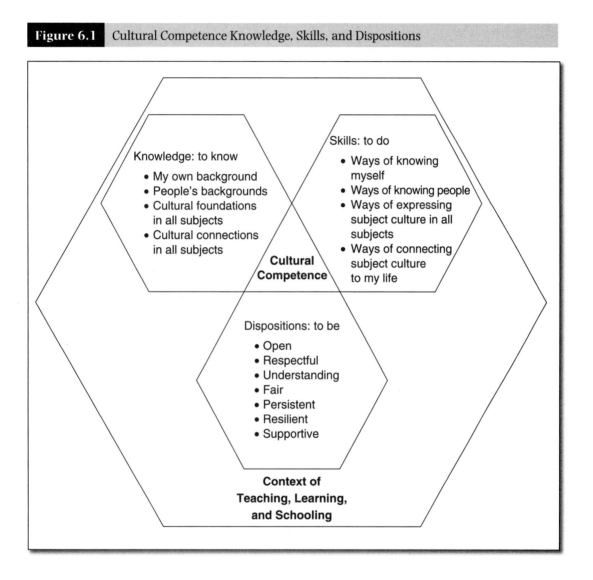

7. Have you selected a variety of instructional strategies to allow each student to understand, connect with, and express learning within each student's cultural background and academic strength?

8. Have you selected a variety of assessment techniques to allow each student to understand, connect with, and express learning within each student's cultural background and academic strength?

9. Have you incorporated opportunities for your students to participate in the selection of materials and assessment techniques?

10. Have you allowed for students to collaborate with other students, both like and unlike themselves, to achieve a variety of learning outcomes?

CREATE A STUDENT-CENTERED AND LEARNER-DRIVEN CLASSROOM

Collaborating and constructing with your students is vital for everyone's success and satisfaction. The first step is to create a student-centered classroom where every student feels like the most important one in the room. Chapter 4 emphasized looking at the community through the eyes of your students. Now, consider your classroom through your students' thoughts and feelings. As you begin to refer to the physical space as "our" classroom, transform the focus so the students own mental and emotional space too.

Examine your curriculum, instruction, and assessments carefully. Are they aligned so each component fulfills the purposes of the other two components? If you begin with the end, can you work your way backward to reach the start? And if you begin in the middle, does each end fit appropriately? Align your plans from multiple perspectives to allow students with various learning styles, strengths, and interests to express their outcomes too. Be careful not to limit your alignment to the needs of a few students.

Think about your integrated units of learning. Do all parts drawn from across the curriculum fit together naturally and holistically? Do the objectives and activities make sense, or have some parts been forced so the entire curriculum is both represented and covered? It is essential for your units of learning to replicate authentic learning. To be authentic, the learning must reflect each student's cultural characteristics. Offering students choices ensures individuality.

Consider your curriculum flow throughout the entire school year. Have you sequenced concepts, processes, and vocabulary so everything builds upon prior learning? Scaffolding so new learning is well supported is vital for the new learning to stand on its own. Likewise, when you spiral back to bring prior learning into focus again, will your students recall and apply the past learning competently and confidently? Some of your students may miss part of the instruction. Devise plans for students to be responsible for their own learning, especially when they are not present.

All of these considerations reflect a student-centered classroom where you have planned and prepared with such breadth and depth that students are excited, engaged, if not completely engrossed in their learning. Your goal is for your students to want to learn more and to share their discoveries with their friends and family.

Student-centered classrooms result in learner-driven outcomes. Think of it like this: if you place a student in the driver's seat, the student determines where the vehicle travels. As you plan your units of learning, ask your students what they want to learn, how they want to learn it, and ways they want to share their learning with one another and their families. Many times, the students are telling you whether you ask them or not. You simply need to listen to them, all of them.

Start constructing menus so the students have choices. Again, you can ask your students what choices to place on the menu. Here is an example for a fourth grade learning unit with the theme of self-discovery. The fourth graders generated the ideas.

Literacy

Identify six different books with self-discovery themes at various levels of difficulty and form book clubs. Students must join one of the book clubs and select one project to demonstrate comprehension of the book. The project choices include:

- Write and present a skit from the book.
- Write and share a set of storyboards summarizing the book.
- Write and discuss an alternative ending to the book.
- Write and draw five significant scenes that take place throughout the book.
- Write and read a letter, speech, or poem that the author might have written.
- Write a conversation that you might have with one of the main characters in the book.

Math and Science; Health and Physical Education

- Keep a journal of one's foods for three weeks to note patterns.
- Calculate the nutritional value of one's food.
- Calculate the health benefits of one's food.
- Keep an exercise log.
- Calculate the health benefits of one's exercise.

Social Studies

- Sketch a map of your favorite places.
- Write several journal entries reflecting on various events and encounters.
- Analyze the journal entries for socialization patterns.
- Write goals for improving study skills and increasing achievement levels.
- Interview a family member or family friend for guidelines to enhance success.

INCORPORATE FAMILIES

Collaboration and construction involve families, especially in Grade K–5 classrooms. To realize each student's complete situation, you need to meet with and know your students' families. You cannot complete the picture until you have met with families to glean more information regarding the students' cultural backgrounds and academic insights.

You may meet families at the usual back-to-school night and open house events, but your time will be limited to visit with each family. Some recommendations for expanding your interaction with families include:

1. Send a note home with your students telling families that you will be calling each one to introduce yourself. Divide the note so a portion can be returned to you. Ask families to provide the name, relationship, telephone number, and time for you to call. Be persistent, as some family members may be reluctant to communicate with you. Some family members may not consider school and teachers positively. Their prior communications have perhaps been focused on problems that they were expected to fix. Also, be flexible. Family members may not be able to talk with you until later in the evening, after work and dinner.

2. Invite families to visit with you at school and at a mutually acceptable time early in the school year as you become acquainted with each student. Explain clearly that this type of conference is a goal-setting conference so everyone can work together to establish academic and social expectations for the school year.

3. Send families a form to complete, seeking information about their work, hobbies, and interests so you can incorporate such information into your curriculum and schedule opportunities for them to share in the classroom. Most students in the early grades are pleased when their family members visit the school and share something special about their family.

4. Schedule one day a week when family members can eat lunch with their children. You can meet the family and visit for a few minutes at the end of the lunch period.

5. Organize a schoolwide event where you can visit with families casually, such as a fall festival. Rather than focusing on the academics, teachers and families can interact as a community and get to know one another better.

FEATURE STUDENT-LED CONFERENCES

One of the most innovative suggestions to enhance everyone's self-efficacy is to incorporate student-led conferences. During a student-led conference, each student reports individual progress to family members, along with the steps the student needs to take to improve individual learning and socialization. This is highly valuable experience. Individual students must accept complete responsibility for their own understandings and accomplishments.

Begin the process on the first day of school by establishing with students that they will be accountable not only for their progress, but also for communicating their progress to their family members at their spring teacher-parent-student conferences. Provide students with a copy of the report form, and introduce each part of the curriculum and instruction that is routinely reported to family members during the spring conferences.

To preview this event, several months ahead, present a mock student-led conference to the students with you playing the role of the student. This mock conference is not only entertaining; it also captures students' attention as they begin to comprehend that they will be evaluating their own progress to their family members.

Throughout the school year, have the students maintain portfolios where samples of their work are kept for the future student-led conference. As the date approaches, allow the students to practice their conferences by conducting fake conferences with their friends. As you observe, the students should reference the report form and tell the listener about their progress supported with various documents as evidence. Remarkably, students realize the areas where they have shown the greatest growth and the areas that need additional attention and energy. The student-led conference also provides a platform that helps bond students with their family members. Family members from all cultural backgrounds recognize and reinforce the hard work and keen insights that their children share with them. Instilling responsibility in young people is admired in all cultures.

MODEL RESILIENCE

As with any endeavor to change and grow, you will encounter resistance from various sources. As you seek and engage in collaboration and construction of new approaches in teaching and learning, you will discover that some of your colleagues and perhaps even your students may express reluctance to go along with your transformation. Family members may view your approaches as trendy and flashy.

As you strive for a student-centered and learner-driven classroom, working with families and colleagues, you must overcome resistance with resilience. Remain flexible yet strong, so you can cope with change and welcome new adventures. Acquiring a sense of resilience will serve you extremely well. You will find yourself seeking new opportunities, engaging in novel activities, and enjoying teaching and living much more than you either anticipated or have enjoyed in the past.

MAP YOUR CHANGES . . .

Collaborating with your colleagues may happen naturally or you may need to give it your concerted effort. Aim for your administrators, colleagues, students, and their families to see you as an effective team player. You may not agree or even like your colleagues, yet you share the mission of providing the best educational setting for a particular group of students. Therefore, you need to map your changes.

Start by selecting one colleague with whom you work every day, and establish a time when you can develop curriculum. Be ready to give as much as you want to get, even if you are a novice teacher. You must enter this relationship equitably. Novices bring many new ideas and resources. Perhaps you are more advanced technologically and you can trade your expertise for another's experiences. View yourself as an equal professional regardless of age and experience.

Begin meeting on a regular basis and include more members of your team. Again, dividing the work helps everyone. Although you might begin by focusing on the tasks, you should soon expand the conversations to reach one another socially.

Repeat the same approaches with other groups of teachers, such as the special area teachers, creating opportunities to collaborate with the music, art, physical education, library, and technology teachers to integrate the curriculum.

Extending Activities for Teachers

1. Tell your school administrator or department chair that you are interested in cultural competence and infusing more cultural competence into your classroom. Ask the administrator if there is another teacher in the school or at another school who also might be interested in cultural competence so you can talk with that individual, and perhaps form a group of educators interested in seeking more information and supporting one another in navigating cultural competence.

2. Visit the children's section of a local library or bookstore to find literature that communicates and exemplifies cultural competence. After reading the literature, decide where to infuse the literature across the curriculum to share it with your students. By sharing the literature in ways that are natural and holistic, the students will view cultural competence as authentic.

3. Visit a teachers' supply store to find curriculum guides and instructional materials to enhance your construction of cultural competence approaches and activities, especially those related to the cultural backgrounds of your students and their families.

4. Examine your curriculum, instruction, and assessments from the perspectives of your students who are first- or second-generation immigrants. Ask them for honest feedback.

5. Invite a colleague into your classroom to observe you and give you feedback.

Extending Activities for Young Learners

Each of these activities should be modified for nonreaders, special education students, and English language learners as developmentally appropriate by using pictures instead of words, providing words for students to select instead of asking students to generate new words, listing possible vocabulary choices on the board, collaborating with learning assistants, and so forth.

1. Find children's literature that emphasizes cultural competence to correlate with all academic subject areas of your grade level. Ask students to draw pictures or write stories showing the similarities and differences between the literature and their lives.

2. Invite family members to visit your classroom to talk about their various cultural backgrounds.

3. Create a place in the classroom to feature one or two students each week. Provide enough time for each student to talk, show artifacts, and answer other students' questions. Guide students in the appropriate techniques for asking personal questions.

4. Combine the students in your classroom with the students in another classroom to collaborate on a special academic or service project.

5. Establish a rotating roster of classroom leaders so each student works with another leader, with each set of partners taking responsibility for a different part of the classroom.

Ivan is a White, European American, lower-middle class, Christian, single man who has been teaching fourth grade for eleven years. He immigrated to the United States from Scotland as a young adult; however, he had no savings when he arrived in the country, so his financial situation has remained difficult.

Ivan is keenly aware of the cultural biases that many immigrants experience. Although he speaks with a Scottish accent that mesmerizes everyone around him, he acknowledges that being White affords him opportunities that many immigrants from other countries do not receive. At times, he overhears his colleagues talking about immigrant students in ways that are not fair and accepting. Ivan has learned that, with some colleagues, he can initiate controversial conversations about being an immigrant by asking leading questions, hoping to prompt these colleagues to rethink their dispositions. With other colleagues with whom he is more comfortable, Ivan can be more direct and tell them his opinions.

Additionally, due to his relative newness to the United States, Ivan is still unfamiliar with some of the history and customs of the country, especially nuanced practices. He must study the curriculum carefully to ensure that his teaching offers breadth, depth, and multiple contexts. His goal is to build upon the state mandates to show equity in all of the knowledge and skills for which he is responsible. Frequently he creates cooperative learning groups, and assigns various perspectives of a topic or issue to the groups of students to research, present, and debate within the classroom. Ivan's students and their families appreciate his approaches for engaging the students in opportunities for exploring diversity of thoughts, beliefs, and actions.

S: Spark Conversation and Climate and SW: Strengthen and Weave Together Complexities and Controversies

7

Navigating cultural competence abounds with many different and conflicting beliefs, and due to the complex and controversial nature of human existence, divergent approaches and conversations accompany these beliefs (Anderson, 1996). Everyone seems to have an opinion on what people should think and how they should interact—especially in classrooms and schools. Initially it may appear overwhelming to map your journey through this aspect of cultural competence, which many teachers perceive to be the most difficult.

However, it is essential to create a community of teaching and learning that provides tools and techniques to inform and support the learners; this climate will ignite with your conversations and model cultural competence, offering guidance and reinforcement for everyone. This chapter is organized around ten foundational strategies for you to consider, conform to your own situation, and then connect to your personal, professional, and pedagogical styles. Although each of these two compass points addresses distinct guidelines, the two compass points are combined, as they inform and support one another sensibly. As you "Spark conversation and climate," S on the Gallavan cultural competence compass, it is also important to move SW, "Strengthen and Weave together the complexities and controversies" associated with navigating cultural competence effectively.

ASSESS EXPECTATIONS

Teachers tend to fall into one of three groups: (1) teachers who want to engage their students in issues and actions related to democratic principles, human rights, educational equity, and social justice at every chance; (2) teachers who view complexities and controversies as conflict and avoid all three at all costs; and (3) teachers who capture the teachable moments when cultural competence fits into the curricular content, pedagogical practices, and sociocultural context. It is essential to know yourself and your multiple audiences so you can enjoy your teaching today and for many days into the future.

Thus, the first step is to assess the content expectations on your teaching team, at your school, within your district, in your state, and from your subject area as stated by the national professional learned society and researchers who are experts in your field. Every field is complex and includes controversial topics, issues, and approaches. For example, when you teach reading, the plot of every story has different viewpoints. There may not even be a concrete ending; the readers are expected to draw their own conclusions. When you teach math, you aim to help your students understand that there are various ways to solve a problem, and also that they are expected to learn various ways to solve every problem. The same expectation applies to science and social studies, where you avoid communicating to your students that there is one right or one best way to think or to demonstrate learning.

Your curriculum overflows with cultural competence; look at the various documents that you are required to follow as you design your plans. You will find criteria that address knowing your students' backgrounds academically and culturally. In order to prepare your learning environment and instructional activities, you have to know your learners. Immediately you encounter complexities as no class is filled with a room of identical students. Now is the time to notice everyone's cultural characteristics and check your own outlooks and attitudes.

Assessing expectations also means knowing your curriculum and content. Here again you find many items related to, if not immersed in, cultural complexities and controversies. You are expected to help every student connect with the learning and achieve success, especially special education and English language learners (Ward & Ward, 2003). As you design your plans, visualize the content through the eyes and experiences of your various learners.

Then establish a learning community so all learners feel safe, are motivated to engage in the learning, and are encouraged to express their discoveries and share their outcomes. As you coconstruct new knowledge and spark conversations with your students, you encounter complexities and controversy in every part of every day.

Most school districts provide teachers with various frameworks for guidance. It is your task to fulfill the expectations by responsibly incorporating the requirements into your curriculum, instruction, assessments, and classroom management.

RECOGNIZE CONTEXT

To fulfill the expectations and make your classrooms successful, it is essential to know your audience well. Students will be far more engaged in the learning and achieve greater outcomes when they are given ownership in the learning process and products. This means offering your students voice or opportunities to talk, along with choices or options in their productivity. This means offering your students voice or opportunities to talk, along with choices or options for expressing their discoveries to demonstrate their productivity.

Giving your students ownership does not mean that you will lose control. It means just the opposite. When your students can talk freely about the learning and select the ways they will express their learning, they become more responsible. With voice and choice come complexity and controversy. Your classroom context then becomes alive and vibrant.

Usually when teachers talk less and listen more, their students begin to engage in conversations. Perhaps on their own or with a little nudging from you, the students will start to explore topics and issues from multiple perspectives. You can pose open-ended questions for students to discuss with partners or in small groups; then they can report their findings to the whole group. Conversations may occur rather casually as students work on various projects, or the discussions may be more direct and purposeful. Understanding the context of your content and community are key elements.

ESTABLISH BOUNDARIES

Encouraging your students to explore topics and issues from multiple perspectives—and to express their learning via self-directed and self-selected outcomes—may appear chaotic to some classroom teachers and school administrators. Frequently new teachers are reticent to adapt these techniques for fear of losing control.

When introducing complex thinking into a class conversation, it is important to establish some boundaries or ground rules. Constructing a list of boundaries collaboratively with your community of learners will encourage everyone to participate in the process and buy into the product. The following list of boundaries provides ideas upon which the students can adjust or build:

1. Listen carefully to the question or topic presented by the teacher or another student.

2. Take a little time to think about your beliefs before you answer the question or talk about the topic.

3. Listen carefully as all other students share their beliefs and thoughts.

4. Stay focused on the primary question or topic, even if another student's comment seems more important, unless other rules have been established allowing students to talk about any part of the conversation at any time.

5. Keep your hands down while other students are talking.

6. Wait your turn; do not talk without being called upon to speak.

7. Consider the question or topic from another viewpoint that is unlike your own viewpoint. You may say, "From another viewpoint, I think that maybe . . ."

8. Remain logical, descriptive, and objective. Give examples stated as "Some people . . ." rather than stating actual names of people whom everyone may know.

9. Stay calm during discussions, especially when you strongly agree or strongly disagree with the speaker. The discussion should not become competitive or confrontational. This is not about winning and losing.

10. Try to identify a viewpoint that is new and unlike your own initial viewpoint.

11. Listen carefully to each expressed viewpoint and consider it in the context of the viewpoint, rather than jump to a conclusion based on either the topic or the speaker. Remember that all conversations are controversial because they feature diverse viewpoints.

12. Keep in mind that the conversation is a sharing of ideas. The ideas may or may not represent how a person thinks, feels, speaks, and acts in all parts of the person's life.

Topics and issues associated with cultural competence involve complex and controversial conversations that teachers want both to encourage and control. Teachers therefore must guide their students to be mindful of their words and messages so students can express their opinions without hurting one another with their words and the tone of their language. For example, if the class is discussing the qualities of an effective president, students should provide specific qualities. Students should not give a president's name as representing effectiveness or ineffectiveness in one giant sweep.

ACCEPT COMPLEXITIES AS OPPORTUNITIES

For many teachers, the best part of teaching may be helping the students create order from what appears to them to be complex. As students solve the pieces of a large puzzle, metaphorically speaking, the students' eyes brighten and smiles jump across their faces. Teachers, then, need to view complex situations as authentic opportunities to teach their students about critical thinking, problem solving, and decision making.

All topics and issues associated with cultural competence are complex. Do not shy away from these conversations. Your students want and need you to guide them through the processes of identifying the parts of the topic or issue, giving them a chance to explore multiple perspectives related to the topic or issue, and to connect the topic or issue to their lives.

Most of your students will have heard their family members or friends talk about some of the topics and issues that you might discuss in class. However, their understanding will likely be extremely limited or biased. Life and complexities are synonymous. By teaching them the steps of identifying the problem, exploring various viewpoints, considering alternate solutions, and analyzing their impacts, you will equip your students with skills they can use in all academic subject areas and throughout their lives.

INTEGRATE COMPLEXITIES INTO CONTENT

It is not difficult to integrate complex topics and issues related to cultural competence into all of your curricular content (Asher, 2007). For example, when you teach language arts, you feature literature and communication via reading, writing, speaking, listening, and viewing. All literature, regardless of its format and genre, includes a plot and characters facing a dilemma. The dilemma is both complex and controversial or it wouldn't be a dilemma. The literature provides the catalyst to identify the problem, explore various viewpoints, consider alternate solutions, and analyze their impacts. If you are given choices in your literature selections, talk with your librarian or look at websites that describe the plots in order to capitalize upon the cultural competence that you want to explore with your students.

The language arts also include writing with mechanics of communication and expressions of creativity. Here you can introduce various writing formats to provide your students with models that may connect with their cultural backgrounds and writing styles. Through writing, students can express their perspectives and share their products with one another.

At first glance, math may appear to be complex but not with complexities associated with cultural competence. However, math strongly links with culture. Consider the various cultural characteristics introduced in Chapter 1. All of us connect with math and apply math to our lives uniquely based on our cultural characteristics. The math concepts may be placed in a context or the computation may be understood based on our cultural characteristics. Additionally, some students, particularly females and students of color, feel less competent and confident in math classes. Teachers need to be aware of all three conditions so they can design instructional strategies to fit all of their students so they connect math culturally, contextualize math computations culturally, and become more competent and confident with math overall.

Science, like math, tends to be viewed as a field that females and students of color may not understand, appreciate, or conquer. Using the same suggestions as presented for teaching math, teachers of science must allow all students time to manipulate the tools so everyone, regardless of one's past experiences, can achieve success. The field of science is perceived to be complex; your task is to simplify the content so all students can understand it.

Social studies are similar to language arts. The content is another form of literature that all students need to know so all students learn about all other students from historical, geographical, economic, and civic perspectives both nationally and internationally. Social studies are the glue that holds the content together. When teaching math, the word problems—sometimes both complex and controversial—contain the context for calculating the problem. When teaching science, every problem that involves human beings becomes a social studies challenge charged with complexities and controversies. Again, do not avoid these opportunities to teach your students to think and to enjoy thinking.

INCLUDE CONTROVERSY INTO MANAGEMENT

It is no surprise that classroom management is complex and controversial; however, being encouraged to include controversy into your classroom management may come as a surprise However, there is no better way to teach critical thinking, problem solving, and decision making, for the situations that arise in your classroom are your students' daily lives.

When you have students who will not fulfill your expectations, in general, the controversy impacts everyone. You have established classroom expectations, perhaps called "rules," that are posted for everyone to see. Likewise, you have established rewards and consequences that accompany compliance and lack of compliance. The students want to see you fulfill your promise of reward and consequence. This exchange teaches them many lessons that apply to learning and living. Yet, you realize that not every breach of the expectations should result in a negative consequence.

There are special situations all the time. Your students benefit when they witness you processing these situations. You want to be fair, yet you also want to show respect in your rapport with your students. For example, you may have a student who is late to class after recess one day. Perhaps this results in the student missing some recess time. However, you examine the situation to discover that this student was asked to return some playground equipment to the gym for another teacher. The situation is excused. You certainly could speak to the student quietly and move quickly to the next academic subject. Or you could take a moment to let all the students know the situation and the conditions associated with the situation, pointing out the controversy and the complexities in your classroom management. Additionally, to prevent students from generating reasons to be late, you would emphasize that this situation was unique and that the other teacher will check with you in the future.

You can use an authentic situation from your classroom, or you can create fictitious situations for your students to solve. As young students mature, with your guidance, they will understand that the expectations are a guideline and that situations prompt all of us to think about the complexities and controversies carefully.

SEIZE THE TEACHABLE MOMENT

Many opportunities to infuse complex and controversial conversations into your classroom will simply present themselves in the curricular content, student connections, and classroom management. You can then decide if you are willing to pursue them, and at what moment. Most likely, this split-second decision will relate to your comfort with leaving the plan and entering the potential conversation. You will need to determine if the topic or issue is one with which you are familiar and comfortable.

It is also important to consider if the topic or issue is one that can be addressed in the time allotted with a sense of closure, or if you will be opening a conversation that seems unending and, perhaps, a bit disconcerting for your students to comprehend. Additionally, it will be helpful to weigh the possibility of underlying agendas. Sometimes students ask questions simply to get the teacher off the plan, upset another student, or advocate a personal agenda. You will need to be extremely careful that students do not express their opinions in ways that communicate personal attacks on other students.

If you want to capture the teachable moment, be sure that all of your students follow your lead. Be clear in establishing that an interesting question or comment has arisen and that you are taking this time to discuss it. Write the topic or issue on the board so everyone can see the words. List some vocabulary words associated with the topic or issue to broaden the understanding. Some of your students may not connect with the original words but they will identify with associated vocabulary.

In addition, list some of the perspectives associated with the topic or issue. Since you are digressing from the prior lesson, you need to immerse your students into the complexities. Ask them to contribute their knowledge and experiences so they make meaningful connections. For example, if your class is examining the variables contributing to a historical event and you have identified several significant subheadings, then you could ask your students to contribute the information that they know or believe related to each subheading. From this list, ask your students what they want to know about each subheading. At this point, you will have to decide the direction of your future teaching and learning. You may discover that the teachable moment becomes much more powerful than the planned learning and you will need to rewrite your future lesson plans.

ENCOURAGE HIGHER-ORDER CRITICAL THINKING

Complex and controversial topics and issues related to cultural competence require higher-order critical thinking due to the multiple perspectives associated with the topics and issues. In addition to the questions requiring students to recall people, places, and events, ask your students questions that prompt them to analyze, compare, contrast, infer, and evaluate so they can provide rationales for and against situations and solutions.

Thinking should be taught to young learners in ways that validate their current thinking, build upon logical intelligence, expand their imaginations, and encourage realistic possibilities (Resnick, 1987). Explain to your students that critical thinking is not easy and requires asking many questions. Allow them opportunities to be challenged, and provide them with freedom to experience thinking that yields multiple solutions, rather than leading them to prescriptive outcomes, specified in advance of the conversation.

Ideas must be considered without judgment yet accepted as accompanied by uncertainty until each student derives individual meaning.

Critical thinking is the perfect link for cultural competence. Not only does every student think differently, but each student thinks about self-selected information and makes unique connections. Allowing your students to express themselves through questions and conversations teaches them to think, value one another, and understand the complexity of the world around them.

PRACTICE PROBLEM SOLVING AND DECISION MAKING

When incorporating problem solving and decision making, you can use an authentic situation from your classroom, or you can create fictitious situations for your students to solve. The key to cultural competence in this area is to value differences in the processes and the products. You may already ascribe to the belief that students learn differently and express their understanding uniquely. However, honestly valuing differences in your classroom through authentic problem solving and decision making may require extra steps. Ten steps to problem solving and decision making with considerations for cultural competence are as follows:

1. Take inventory and decide if there is a problem. Keep in mind that all students will not agree that there is a problem or that there is the same problem.

2. Define the problem(s). All students will not define the same problem or define the problem with the same degree of concern.

3. Look for causes of the problem(s). All students will not identify the same possible causes of the problem; some students will identify people and some students will identify situations or events. Investigate closely when the problem is associated with a person.

4. Brainstorm alternatives for solving the problem(s). Your students will brainstorm many different alternatives, all of which should be considered seriously.

5. Select a possible solution. Determine the procedures to select a possible solution by voting, consensus, or compromise.

6. Plan the solution. Divide the class into small groups to construct plans.

7. Test the solution on a small scale. Allow each group to test their own plans to solve the problem.

8. Analyze the results of the test. Each group can report their own results to the whole group.

9. Determine if the results are acceptable. Connect the acceptability of the results with cultural competence.

10. Implement the solution on a larger scale. Continue checking for cultural competence in other subject areas and with other themes throughout the school year.

The steps of problem solving and decision making are as important as the outcomes. Some students will be more attentive to the steps and some students will be more attuned to the outcomes. These are cultural differences. Cultural differences impact learning styles too.

EXAMINE RATIONALITY

The outcomes of problem solving and decision making are judged by their degree of rationality (Oakley, 1997). Yet, due to the presence of human differences, rationality is an inconsistent quality that is culturally based. Each one of us determines, through our individual value systems, what is considered rational. An outcome may sound good in theory but not be practical. Similarly, an outcome may be one that an individual supports due primarily to one's values and not due to theory or practicality. Individuals define rationality informally and institutions define it formally. And too often, institutions operate according to complicated sets of rules and regulations that overpower all other rationality.

Engagement in problem solving and decision making involves rationality. Through each step of problem solving, students must be prompted to consider rational thinking from multiple perspectives. Be conscious to not fall prey to tokenism by asking one girl to represent the voice of all girls or one Hispanic to represent the voice of all Hispanics. Instead, contextualize rationality as an intricate force within each person that has multiple cultural characteristics.

PRACTICE CONSCIENTIZATION . . .

Conscientization is a Portuguese word that means critical consciousness, developed by Paulo Freire (1970); it is a social concept that focuses on acquiring an in-depth understanding of the world from multiple perspectives. Some of the perspectives will be new and even contradictory to known and accepted perspectives.

Conscientization empowers students by examining with them what is most important or critical to various individuals and groups in the present, the past, and into the future. The goal of this form of examination is to place the student into a transformative consciousness that prompts research, conversation, and identification. Ultimately, the student moves into a state of social actions, thus achieving a sense of freedom for underrepresented and oppressed populations.

The concept of conscientization is captured in the saying that "you can give people fish so the people can eat, or you can teach people to fish so the people can feed themselves." Through culturally based conversations, which by description are complex and controversial, you guide your students as they dig deep, collaboratively, into both the content and the practices to coconstruct knowledge and make valuable connections through your classroom experiences.

Extending Activities for Teachers

1. Make a list of some controversial topics and issues related to your major units of learning that you might integrate into your curriculum and instruction. Talk with an experienced teacher or your department chair about techniques for introducing controversial topics and issues into the classroom. Select one technique to try with your next unit of learning. Evaluate your effectiveness, insert improvements, and try it again with another unit of learning. Most likely, you will discover that these exercises become the motivation that your students are seeking to engage in your content.

2. Record lists of complex and controversial topics and issues that other teachers incorporate into their classrooms to build a selection from which you can choose as you develop your curriculum. You may discover that many of the topics and issues relate to one another through a reoccurring theme. For example, one fourth grade teacher teaches many different body systems in her science classes. Her ongoing theme became the costs of taking care of oneself. The class examined the costs of food, exercise, medicine, and so forth. The theme expanded into her social studies classes as the students began to realize that not everyone has the same information, access, and opportunities.

3. All teachers have encountered a situation when a student has raised a question or made a statement related to a controversial topic and issue. To be ready for these situations, find a trusted colleague and practice the conversation in advance. Your preparation will equip you with the vocabulary to sound intelligent and the

mechanisms to positively acknowledge the question, answer it briefly, and not let it usurp your day's lesson. If you allow the question to become the lesson, some of your students will recognize that you can be taken off the subject easily. You want to maintain control of the conversation.

4. Take advantage of the many different local seminars or public television programs that are available to inform you about topics and issues that are new or unclear to you. Every one of us has much to learn, and the more we understand, the more effective we are as teachers of our content areas, especially in making cultural connections for each of our students.

5. Similarly, read a newspaper or news magazine so you glean local, national, and global reports especially related to cultural competence. It is important to stay informed and ahead of your students, and to be ready if a student shares an observation or asks you a question. If a question arises, and you do not know the answer, be willing to say you do not know and that you will find out more information and get back to the class.

Extending Activities for Young Learners

Each of these activities should be modified for nonreaders, special education students, and English language learners as developmentally appropriate by using pictures instead of words, providing words for students to select instead of asking students to generate new words, listing possible vocabulary choices on the board, collaborating with learning assistants, and so forth.

1. Play the game of knots by placing students into groups of no more than six players. Students stretch their arms out in front of them and grab the hands of two other people. Students should not hold hands as a pair nor should students hold hands with the person standing to their immediate left or right. The goal is then to create a circle with all students holding hands with the person standing to their immediate left and right. Therefore, the task is to lift linked hands over students' heads or to step over linked hands to unravel the knot. The purpose of this game is to help students see that they can work together to make complex situations much more simple.

2. Draw a large T-chart on the board and give students individual copies of a T-chart. The left side of the T should be labeled "Words" and the right side of the T-chart should be labeled "Actions." With the group,

list a word on the left and ask the class to elicit corresponding actions. For example, the word might be "thinking" and the actions might be quiet, fast, or slow (depending on the situation), in your head, searching, calculating, and so forth. The purpose of the charts is to identify specific actions that correspond to words that are frequently used during teaching and learning, especially during problem solving and decision making. Some of the students' actions will be different based on cultural characteristics; these words need to be shared and respected by all members of the class.

3. Select a controversial issue for your students to debate. Consider the issue carefully so it is developmentally appropriate for your students and fits into your school's culture. You may want to discuss your selected issue with your mentor or department chair in advance of organizing the debate. Then divide the class into various factions representing the corresponding number of viewpoints. You may want to select the groups in advance or let your students draw names from a basket. Allow each group to present three facts to substantiate their view and three facts to use to respond to other groups' facts. In addition, before the debate starts, decide if you want to close the debate with a solution or leave it unanswered.

4. Borrow the game Apples to Apples. This is a game that includes decks of cards with words printed on them. The student who is "it" selects a green apple card from the pile. Everyone else selects one of the red apple cards. Students select on the premise that their card connects with the word on the green card. Then the person who is it decides which of the red apple word cards best exemplifies the word on the green apple card. There are no right or wrong answers; the students make their own cultural connections. Great amounts of conversations and laughter accompany this game as students explain their rationale.

5. Divide the class into groups of no more than ten students in each group. Place one long strip of masking tape on the floor for each group of students. The strip of tape should be approximately thirty feet. (You can also play this game in the gym or on the basketball court using the lines painted on the court.) Ask ten students to stand on each line, and tell students that there is no talking during the game. The task is for students to move on each line, communicating with sign language, so they are standing in order of their birthdays during a calendar year, January through December. During the process, students must keep one foot on the tape at all times. Students have to climb over, under, or around one another to place all members of the group in the correct order. The purpose of this game is to experience new ways of problem solving.

Madison is finishing her first year teaching second grade. She completed her internship in second grade and she feels good about her accomplishments. As she begins the fourth quarter of the school year, Madison wants to instill more compassion among her students, so she decides to challenge them with some changes. The school recently adopted service learning and Madison is eager to incorporate these activities into her classroom.

Madison shares her proposal with the class at the next classroom meeting. The students seem receptive so Madison suggests that the class work in small groups of triads to brainstorm projects. Before forming groups, Madison facilitates a class conversation to establish some guidelines. Since they have no financial resources, the class recommends that they spend as little money as possible, and that they visit a location during the school day and within walking distance of the school.

When the groups are ready to report, brainstormed projects include cleaning up the neighborhood park, volunteering in the early childhood center located at their school, visiting the nearby senior citizen care facility, and helping in either the school or community library. With all of the projects listed on the board, Madison gives the students ballots so they can vote secretly and determine one project for the class.

The class lists questions that they need to answer before embarking upon the project. Then Madison gives each group a large sheet of paper, and the group members generate possible answers to their questions.

Throughout this process, Madison not only works collaboratively with the students, she increases their commitment to cultural competence through a fascinating challenge. As the students continue preparing their project, Madison will integrate academic activities to increase the students' compassion and comprehension of service learning to promote change.

W: Waken Compassion and Commitment and NW: Nurture and Welcome Challenges and Changes

8

This chapter combines feelings with actions. Compassion involves strong feelings of care and concern for another person, particularly one who is suffering from misfortune. However, compassion remains distant and passive until one expresses commitment. Commitment is the pledge or promise to take action to provide assistance.

Most teachers experience a great amount of compassion. This disposition may be one of the more compelling reasons that people become teachers and stay in the profession. Teachers also want to teach compassion to their students. A general outlook sweeping across U.S. society today is that people do not seem to care about one another. Many teachers want to revitalize feelings of care for one another and for all people and parts of the planet Earth.

Making compassion come to life and become meaningful for students requires the commitment to take action. Commitment manifests in many different ways that include higher order and critical thinking, problem solving, decision making, accomplished deeds, and responsible obligation. This chapter provides you with step-by-step procedures for introducing compassion and commitment into your classroom as part of your curriculum to bring challenge and change.

As you complete your journey around the Gallavan cultural competence compass, you will discover that these two compass points should be considered both independently and together as one major thrust. "Waking compassion and commitment," W on the compass, must be accompanied by taking action; arousing awareness presents the optimal opportunity to make a difference by "Nurturing and Welcoming challenges and making changes" in ourselves and the world around us.

UNDERSTAND THE CONCEPT OF CARE

The concept of care is somewhat abstract, elusive, and, at times, a paradox. Care involves giving various amounts and types of attention to another person or groups of people. The attention can range from close constant attention, as in taking care of an infant or a sick person, to being aware of a situation and checking on it occasionally, as in maintaining an adult friendship. Attention can range from immediate and intense, as in an emergency, to long term and ongoing, as in a student project in your classroom. There are times that care seems to be a distant thought or a low-key awareness about a situation, and there are times that care becomes a focused attention accompanied by a flurry of activity related to a specific project and outcome. Given the context of the situation, the amounts and types of attention become more specific.

Care also involves several levels of attention. Care can relate to an individual, as in taking care of oneself. Families strive for their children to be able to care for themselves at home just as teachers want their students to take care of themselves at school. Another level is to care for other people. Again, families want their children to care about other members of the family, sharing responsibilities and possessions. Likewise, teachers need students to care about one another in sharing the space and teaching one another in ways that supplement the teacher's approaches.

On a larger scale, care includes everything and everyone around us, including things and people that are not on the immediate horizon. Considering the planet is a shared home, all people must take care of their individual spaces so all other people in the present and future can use and appreciate it too. Herein lies the paradox. Choices that some people make to take care of themselves may or may not result in the same choices that other people or the larger general society would endorse. For example, a student in your classroom may decide that it is in his best interest to help another student with an assignment. While the kind-hearted student should be thanked, you also want the helped student to learn to become more independent. You must tactfully thank and redirect the helpful student to attend to his own work, allowing the helped student to be more independent with the assignment.

This situation demonstrates the paradox of care because the next day, you may ask students to help one another. Now you face the quandary of explaining when it is appropriate to help and when it is appropriate not to help. Many teachers find themselves discussing care with their students in some way almost every day.

The concept of care also becomes complicated as each person seems to possess a different definition of care, ways of demonstrating care, and judgments about other people's degrees of care. Definitions, demonstrations, and judgments about care are culturally based, as each of us develops these qualities from our families, friends, and community role models when we are quite young.

FEATURE COMPASSION IN YOUR CLASSROOM

Compassion starts with awareness of the people in the world near and far, and then showing respect, sensitivity, and care. Generally, compassion is shown for people suffering in pain; these situations pull at our heartstrings more than the feelings of sympathy or empathy. When we are compassionate, we feel the magnitude of the pain and suffering and we want to alleviate the discomfort in appropriate and appreciated thoughts, words, and actions.

Compassion is not pity and should not result in charitable acts contributed without feeling. Many people in U.S. society tend to be charitable without compassion. Likewise, compassion also is not altruism. At times, compassion goes beyond caring to the point of altruism, where one gives of oneself without any thought about receiving. Acts of pure altruism are rare in today's society but the concept of altruism is important to teach in your classroom.

Although your students may begin to identify with care and compassion for other people, one theme to incorporate into your classroom is the ability to respond to anger and violence by withdrawing and staying calm. Your students should be guided away from responding to anger and violence with more anger and violence. When students encounter people and situations that seem to be unfair, words and blows may be exchanged. This is exactly when care and compassion should occur in your classroom. Ideally, students will step back from the miscommunication and recognize that there is no need to escalate the situation with additional bullying and revenge.

In most classroom encounters, a teacher or administrator is required to help students process the situation. However, by teaching care and compassion in your classroom, you may be able to equip your students with the techniques to calm themselves before situations get out of control.

Compassion is an affect that you want to adopt and establish as a foundation in your curriculum. Every part of your curriculum offers opportunity to feature care and compassion. The ideas for infusing care and compassion into your curriculum seem endless. Here are a few suggestions:

- Create fictitious situations for your students to role-play so they can practice the words and actions that will help them with acceptable and unacceptable interactions.
- Find children's literature or movie clips with examples of care and compassion so students read about and see the appropriate interactions displayed by the characters.
- Reference famous people in every content area who showed care and compassion so your students can begin to identify with these various individuals.
- Write quotations about care and compassion on the board. Organize projects at school and in the community for your students to become involved in acts of care and compassion.
- Teach students to show appreciation by saying "thank you" and writing thank-you notes. If you have a guest speaker or any kind of special event or service, include the writing of thank-you notes into every lesson. This act should become a habit of mind.

The most effective way for your student to learn about care and compassion is for you to model care and compassion with all your students. Emphasize, through verbal articulation, that you are demonstrating care and compassion so your students see the concepts in action. Take time when redirecting your students' actions that your concern is based on care and compassion, emphasizing the benefits of feeling care and compassion.

Be kind when speaking about students, other teachers, and school personnel. Some teachers take liberties in talking about their students and colleagues in front of their students. Your students may be too young to understand underlying humor, so be careful with your sarcasm.

Be sure that your words and actions match. Some teachers talk about caring and being compassionate when in reality they are not kind to and supportive of all of their students. You may want to invite a trusted colleague into your classroom to give you honest feedback regarding your interactions with your students, both in the classroom and between classes in the hall, on the way to lunch, and so forth. Some teachers seem to display a different demeanor when they help their students make transitions between classes and activities. You can also keep a journal of your interactions with specific students to analyze your patterns.

Be aware of the roles that cooperation and competition play in your classroom. While some competition is healthy and can raise achievement levels, overuse of competition undermines care and compassion. Your use of competition may support only some of your students and not all of your students. In addition, consider how groups and teams are formed. If you allow students to select their own group members, some students may be overlooked too often. You may also construct groups and place all of the strong students together in one group so you develop new leaders in the rest of the class.

EXAMINE CHALLENGES IN EDUCATION

Education tends to be reactionary; frequently it seems that problems must be solved quickly and efficiently after they have arisen to appease the public. It may appear that the situation is simple to review but overwhelming to reform. Through the years, many attempts have been made to reform our nation's education systems. Navigating cultural competence to achieve efficacy requires understanding the following eight challenges to pursue future changes. Each of the eight challenges aligns with a point on the cultural compass.

First, notice that the population of the United States continues to change over time. This is not a new phenomenon. The nation is and always has been composed of immigrants from many different countries; some immigrants came to the United States by choice, and some were brought here by force (Ogbu, 2000). The nation was established on the beliefs of equality and freedom. Children of immigrants have been attending school since the nation began. Some students were and are welcomed and well educated; some students were and are neither welcomed nor educated. The resulting disparities have become a problem for the nation, and thus, over time, some laws and attitudes have been challenged and changed.

Second, negotiate and evaluate how the nation's school populations have changed. There are increasing numbers of students of color. However, the number of teachers of color has not increased. Approximately 40 percent of students are students of color; however, less than 15 percent of the nation's educators are teachers of color. Achievement rates for students of color have continued to fall steadily, and dropout rates have continued to rise dramatically. Today's school populations do not reflect the nation's populations or their stories.

Third, in establishing context, unfortunately most people like remembering their schools from previous decades when they were students attending schools, rather than examining schools in a contemporary context through the eyes and minds of adults. While memories are fun to share, schools need to be considered in the moment—providing services to today's students who need to prepare for tomorrow's world. Yesterday's schools may not have been as wonderfully rewarding for all students as many people tend to remember them through their fuzzy romantic memories.

Fourth, seeking and engaging conversations for educating a nation of young people is a huge enterprise involving many people, each of whom brings a unique or slightly different view of education's mission, vision, and operation. Decisions have to be made, and decisions with equitable outcomes for this many people are impossible to make fairly.

Fifth, the nation's educational systems and outcomes impact every-one, and sparking conversations encourages everyone to express an opinion on our schools' effectiveness and efficiency. Getting everyone's attention and involvement is both gratifying and troubling. Everyone is not a professional educator or current on the situation in our nation's schools and classrooms, yet almost everyone has attended school or knows someone who attended school, so most people consider themselves to be knowledgeable experts.

Sixth, in order to strengthen and weave together the complexities and controversies, many people—including educators—realize that schools and classrooms must be created so all students feel safe and welcomed, high standards are expected of all students and educators, educators teach all students, and the needs of all students are met. These challenges require more changes in laws and attitudes to write the policies, provide the funding, support the educators, and inform the public (Reeves, 2009).

Seventh, the goal of wakening compassion and commitment has been achieved for many people and educators. However, resistance abounds across the United States, so advocates must become more resilient to ensure efficacy in their work and their communities.

Eighth, the future entails nurturing challenges and changes with your students in your classroom, with your colleagues in your school, with the professional educators in your district, with the members of your various communities, and with the legislators in your state. You can be the change.

CONNECT WITH CULTURAL COMPETENCE

The challenges in education connect directly to cultural competence; sadly, there is a tendency to blame the victim. Many people are unable or unwilling to think that education and life could or should change. There are strong beliefs voiced in words like, "It was good enough for me when I was a kid; it is good enough today," "Why can't they (or those people) do it the way we have always done it here?" and "If you don't like here, go away."

None of these statements make sense, and most people would not want to hear these statements said to or about them; yet words like this are either spoken or acted upon every day across our nation, whether the reference is school or society. Laws and attitudes have changed over time; they will continue to change as new challenges are acknowledged.

As you navigate your personal, professional, and pedagogical existence, cultural competence means doing the right thing because it is the right thing to do. Through your journeys, reflect upon your own thoughts, beliefs, words, actions, and interactions as an individual, as an educator in general, and as a classroom teacher responsible for a particular content with a specific age group of students. Your commitment to welcoming cultural competence into your personal life, professional demeanor, and pedagogical expertise may occur across all three aspects of your existence simultaneously or in discrete steps separated from one another (Pohan & Aguilar, 2001).

To illustrate commitment to cultural competence, now meet Roger. Roger shared that he began by examining his own cultural background and individual cultural characteristics. After reflection, Roger recognized that, being born as a White male into a middle-class family, he was entitled to privileges that other people did not receive. Roger remembers feeling like school was "all about me and my doing well." Roger was a member of a scout troop, a sports team, and several school clubs. He could go anywhere he wanted in his town; people seemed to know him and his family.

Roger wanted to become a teacher to offer his students the same satisfaction he experienced at school. However, as he began his university courses and started visiting schools, he realized that his life was a charmed life, one not shared by everyone. This single discovery strengthened Roger's desire to become a teacher so he could open doors to as many other students as possible.

Many teachers begin acknowledging their challenges and changes the same way that this man transformed through personal reflections and discoveries. Your challenges and changes may be stimulated through your desire to influence the educational system as a professional educator or through your intentions to impact the students in your own classes through your pedagogical expertise.

OVERCOME RESISTANCE

Roger's story continues with his interactions with his colleagues. Roger was satisfied with his efforts to infuse cultural competence in his classroom. However, he encountered resistance among his colleagues. He was surprised when he described his initial successes with incorporating cultural competence into his curriculum by expanding the choice of materials and allowing students more choices in their selection of projects.

Roger anticipated support; however, his colleagues seemed more skeptical and one asked him somewhat sarcastically if he thought he might be wasting his time and the school's money. Roger responded that he had used his allocated money and that time would tell. His main intent was to redirect the conversation altogether, but he realized that he had agitated some of his colleagues.

To advance his professional growth and to develop a support group, Roger enrolled in a graduate course at the local university focused on valuing cultural diversity. In the course, he met other classroom teachers who were traveling his same journey related to cultural competence and they began corresponding electronically.

For a while, Roger continued to encounter occasional defensiveness and resistance among his colleagues. It seemed the more comfortable he became with infusing cultural competence into his classroom, the less comfortable certain colleagues were with him. Roger also noted that the conversations had started to change when he was with his colleagues. The culturally offensive references and so-called humor seemed to end. Shortly thereafter, Roger's colleagues seemed more accepting of him and left him alone.

When Roger met with his school administrator for his annual review, the administrator noted the students' academic and social improvements. Roger explained that he had taken a course in cultural competence and was intrigued with the continued changes. The administrator expressed support by granting Roger additional funds to expand his curriculum. The administrator also asked Roger what changes could be instituted around the school, and Roger suggested that the administrator appoint a committee to start the conversation. This suggestion was accepted and Roger became active in the school's cultural competence committee. The group began meeting regularly and issued a newsletter for teachers to exchange ideas.

TEACH DEMOCRATIC PRINCIPLES

Chapter 1 introduced four overarching goals of cultural competence. Here we place the four goals in the context of challenge and change in your classroom. In a democracy, everyone is accepted, everyone has a vote, and everyone's thoughts and beliefs are honored and respected through accommodation. Your classroom does not operate as a true democracy; however, you can teach about democratic principles, incorporate them into some of your classroom procedures, and create an environment framed on democratic principles (Daffen & Anderson, 2009).

Teaching about democratic principles is essential before practicing them with your students, regardless of the content of your curriculum. Your students should understand not only what you are doing, but why you ascribe to a different set of procedures than the students may have experienced in other classrooms. Then, identify the presence of democratic principles, such as letting each student speak or taking a vote, so students connect the concept with a practice.

Most important, use democratic principles to interact both formally and informally with your students. When your students ask you questions that may be considered complex or controversial, it is important to demonstrate understanding and respond appropriately. Not all of your students' questions need a detailed reply; you may need to acknowledge the question and ask the student to talk with you after class if time does not permit at that moment.

If a student shares a story that may be culturally unique, model acceptance. The same advice relates to the appearance of your students. If your students voice disagreements with one another, you want to help resolve the disagreement through calm dialogue where everyone can speak and be heard.

Your classroom must offer a high-quality education for everyone, multiple perspectives evident across the curricular content, multiple strategies of experiencing and connecting content to personal lives evident in the instruction, multiple techniques for expressing one's progress, and full acceptance and participation in the learning community. The classroom should be one that your students call their own.

ENSURE EDUCATIONAL EQUITY

Now that your classroom follows democratic principles, be sure to practice educational equity. This topic focuses more on your teaching. Here are some difficult questions to ask yourself:

- Are you moving around the classroom so you can connect with each student and give each one an opportunity to talk with you during class? Some teachers tend to stand in the same spot when teaching, then sit down and expect the students to approach them. If you sit, do all of your students feel safe and comfortable meeting at your desk or table?
- Are you spending the same amount of time or an equitable amount of time with each student? Some teachers realize that they spend most of the time with the same students each day and hardly any time with some students. You are encouraged to keep a checklist of

your students and mark how often you interact with each of them formally and informally.

- Do you ask the same types of questions with each student? Do you probe and delve equitably to advance all students' learning? Some teachers will ask follow-up questions with some students and not with other students and for a variety of reasons. Again, keep a checklist and notice your patterns.

- Do you positively reinforce all students with the same enthusiasm? Some teachers prefer some students over other students and thus, these teachers tend to display more support for their preferred students. You want to be sure that all students feel welcomed and wanted.

- Is your humor neutral or is it prejudicial or sarcastic? Some teachers err in thinking that their students will respond to sarcasm. Most likely, your students will not understand your sarcasm and may not trust you when you are sarcastic.

- Are you extending the same opportunities to all students? Some teachers select the same students to participate in special events. These teachers base their selections on academic and social qualities that some students cannot achieve.

- Are you disciplining your students fairly and equitably? Be aware of the students who are punished and how they are punished.

- Are you making references to special services equitably? Note the patterns of which students are referred to special services and the reasons for the referrals.

You may want to review these questions of educational equity on your own practices or you may want to discuss them with a school administrator. There may be some issues that the whole school needs to research and discuss.

CHAMPION HUMAN RIGHTS

Every U.S. citizen is entitled to a set of human rights that must be honored, respected, taught, and modeled in your classroom. You can begin by teaching about the changes in human rights since the founding of the United States. You also can talk about how the United States is a model for the rest of the world and that not all students have the same rights as the students in your classroom.

However, your primary goal is to eradicate bias, discrimination, and stereotyping among your students (Sleeter & McLaren, 2009). Begin by teaching your students about these words and how the connotations are detected in words and actions. There are many selections of children's literature that you can use to introduce this discussion. You also are encouraged to guide your students in using the phrase, "I know someone who . . ." when the students want to tell you what a person you all know says or does. Be conscious not to establish an environment where students report on one another.

You may detect some discrimination in your formal interactions, but more likely, discrimination will become evident during informal interactions. If you have established a safe and welcoming community of learners, your students may repeat words they have heard at home or from their friends. Likewise, you may become aware of discrimination when students are passing out supplies, choosing groups, lining up, and so forth. It is important to watch and listen carefully.

When discrimination occurs, talk with the student individually and supportively. Restate the words or actions so the student can visualize the event. Then tell the student that these words or actions could be considered discrimination and that discrimination is not allowed at school or in society. The student may become defensive and share with you where she heard the words or say that "everyone uses them." You can then review the expectations in your classroom and guide the student in making other choices in words or actions. If there has been an encounter between two students, you may need to speak with both of them at one time so everyone is clear and is treated equitably. As you solve these issues, you model human rights.

PROMOTE SOCIAL JUSTICE

The fourth overarching goal of cultural competence attends to social justice. You rely upon democratic principles to establish your curriculum, instruction, assessments, and management; you manifest educational education through your pedagogical practices. You emphasize human rights in helping your students to interact positively and productively with one another; you promote social justice in creating context and connecting everything from your classroom into the world.

Social justice involves helping every student to become a good citizen and to help fellow students to be good citizens. Through your conversations about social justice, point out that getting along with other people means being able to disagree pleasantly. People should be able to state their opinions at appropriate times and places. Likewise, a person should be able to question an action if the person feels injustice has occurred. Promoting social justice also helps to reduce intimidation and bullying that may occur among your students overtly or covertly in your classroom and around the school. Reading and writing about social justice will empower your students (Christensen, 2000).

COMMIT TO COMMITMENT . . .

The word *commitment* generates a list of descriptors that includes (in alphabetical order) allegiance, assurance, dedication, dependability, duty, faithfulness, loyalty, obligation, pledge, promise, responsibility, and trust. These words capture what some people claim is the single most important characteristic of success.

Most people want commitment from other people, but most people tend to avoid making commitments. We like the flexibility of changing our minds in the moment. This dichotomy does not translate well to your students. Students need to be able to depend on you to learn about making commitments themselves. When you make a commitment to your students, be sure to follow through so your students learn from your words and actions. Like learning about compassion, articulate your actions so your students make strong and lasting connections.

Teaching commitment involves critical thinking, clear communication, problem solving, and decision making to establish a shared or common foundation from which everyone works. Commitment means interacting with all kinds of other people. It also means maintaining self-respect by being honest, showing courage, and developing self-control.

Throughout your curriculum and instruction, capture the teachable moments to highlight individual commitment and acts of public commitment (Giroux, 1988). Your students will benefit greatly when they hear and see commitment as part of literature, movies, and in the lives of researchers in all content areas. Invite guest speakers to visit your classroom to share their stories of commitment to their work and passions.

You are a caring, compassionate, and committed individual or most likely you would not be a teacher. Learning and being motivated to learn also may have occurred rather easily for you. Now you face your classroom of students who may not share in your strengths and passions. You learned these strengths and passions from your role models and experiences. Now it is your turn to provide these opportunities for your students—all of your students. You want to build upon your wisdom to help your students navigate cultural competence too.

Extending Activities for Teachers

1. Compassion and commitment can be achieved with service learning. For ideas, explore websites from the National Service-Learning Clearinghouse: http://www.servicelearning.org/, and the National Service-Learning Partnership: http://www.service-learningpart nership.org/site/PageServer.

2. Talk about service learning with your friends who are parents of children the same age as the students in your classroom. From these discussions, you can glean insights that will help you to organize and carry out your own service learning projects more successfully.

3. Look at your curriculum and brainstorm connections with the community. You may be able to integrate several learning objectives together to make both the learning and the service learning more powerful and effective.

4. Interview a colleague who has organized service learning projects with students the same ages as you teach. Find out about the kind of projects and how involved the students are with the details of the project. If you are planning a service learning project, to maintain the integrity of the project, be well prepared with all aspects of the project, be sure that the project is student centered and learner driven, and that other adults (school administrators and family members) understand your plan.

5. Volunteer at a soup kitchen or similar service so you can experience care and compassion firsthand. If possible, talk with the organizers to hear their stories. Take time to journal your reflections after this experience.

Extending Activities for Young Learners

Each of these activities should be modified for nonreaders, special education students, and English language learners as developmentally appropriate by using pictures instead of words, providing words for students to select instead of asking students to generate new words, listing possible vocabulary choices on the board, collaborating with learning assistants, and so forth.

1. Place your students in groups of no more than five students in each group. Ask each student to list two or three items about which they care or feel compassionate. Then, ask students to share their lists within their small groups. Next ask groups to share their lists with the whole class. The purpose of this activity is to identify and describe the many different items about which your students are compassionate. This exercise also allows you to preassess their understanding of the concept of compassion.

2. Invite a guest speaker, such as a teacher from another classroom or school or a member of the community, into your class to discuss a service learning project. Encourage students to ask questions and make connections to their own lives.

3. Brainstorm a list of various services in the community that help other people. Then place your students in small groups of no more than five students in each group. Ask each group to identify the kinds of help that each service provides people in the community and offer a brief rationale for each service. Ask each group to share with the entire class. Then add information related to other services that were not shared by the groups.

4. Talk with your school librarian to find a book about compassion, such as *Hey Little Ant* by Phillip and Hannah Hoose. Read the book aloud. Then ask students to write individual endings to the story. Let students share their individual endings with a partner; select a few students to share their endings with the entire class.

5. After much preparation, organize a service learning project with your students.

Resource A

Gallavan Cultural Competence Compass

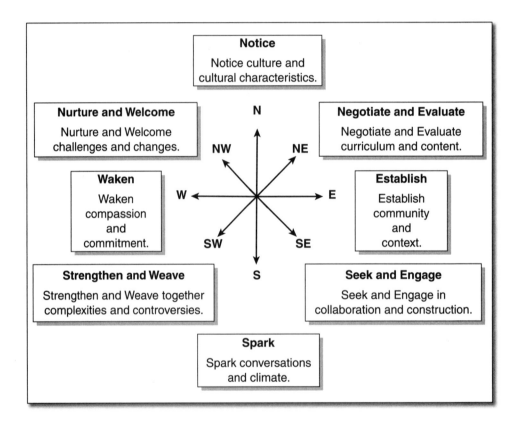

Notice
Notice culture and cultural characteristics.

Nurture and Welcome
Nurture and Welcome challenges and changes.

Negotiate and Evaluate
Negotiate and Evaluate curriculum and content.

Waken
Waken compassion and commitment.

Establish
Establish community and context.

Strengthen and Weave
Strengthen and Weave together complexities and controversies.

Seek and Engage
Seek and Engage in collaboration and construction.

Spark
Spark conversations and climate.

N NW NE W E SW SE S

Resource B

Review Checklist

One day last winter, my sister and I were grappling with a family issue when she summarized our challenge with this philosophical query, "Is asking the questions the same as knowing the answers?" We agreed that most likely, if we were articulating the questions by understanding the situation, then we probably already knew the possible answers.

Our exchange applies to your navigating cultural competence. You know the questions and the answers:

- What do I need to know to infuse cultural competence across my curriculum content? Your curricular content must include the histories, accomplishments, and contributions of all people. Your students need to see themselves as active, valuable, and equally important participants in the content. Your textbook, materials, displays—everything—must ensure cultural competence so all students learn about all students. Your goal is to connect the curriculum to past learning, future learning, other academic disciplines, and, most important, the students' personal lives. You can achieve this goal only by knowing your students' academic and cultural backgrounds and cultural characteristics.
- What do I need to do to infuse cultural competence across my instructional strategies? Your instructional strategies must allow for all learning styles and all forms of multiple intelligences. As you build upon students' strengths, it is necessary to also fortify their weaker areas. That means evaluating, with the particular student, each student's abilities fully. Your instructional strategies must allow students to work independently, with partners, in small groups, and as a whole class. Your goal is to offer a balance of learning environments.
- What do I need to believe to infuse cultural competence across my assessment techniques? Too many teachers overlook their assessment

techniques, possibly because they do not understand what assessment entails, they do not know how to construct appropriate assessments, or they don't care if all of their students demonstrate achievement on their selected assessments. Embedded in your belief that your students can achieve, make sure that you measure not only what you have taught, but also what they have learned. It is important to assess every day, starting with collecting data for a particular unit of learning via preassessments before the teaching and learning begin, formative assessments while teaching and learning occur, and summative assessments after the teaching and learning end. With this, construct all kinds of assessments to measure all levels of learning so students are selecting items, writing responses, relaying information, showing outcomes, and using a combination of all four forms of communication to demonstrate their knowledge, skills, and dispositions based on your knowledge, skills, and dispositions. Students connect with various parts of the curriculum and instruction; they have strengths in various forms of expression. Believe that your students want to showcase their accomplishments through various types of assessments, and then give them permission to achieve, and they will. Assessments begin with your attitudes toward helping all students to succeed.

• What do I need to respect to infuse cultural competence across my classroom management? *Respect* is the key word here. You have to respect each student for every cultural characteristic that the student possesses at the surface, intermittent, and deep levels. You have to respect the learning environment as a shared community of learners. You have to respect that the learning is composed of aligned curriculum, instruction, and assessments, and that the learning is about your students, not you. You have to respect yourself as a change agent committed to cultural competence.

This checklist summarizes the ideas shared with you in this book so you can conduct your own overall review based on the Gallavan cultural competence compass. Five key ideas have been identified for each point on the compass corresponding to two columns. Three of the key ideas apply to your teaching; two key ideas apply to your professional development. One column allows you to record the evidence. The other column allows you to record the plan.

Checklist for Cultural Competence		
Compass Points and Key Ideas	*Evidence*	*Plan*
N: Notice Culture and Cultural Characteristics		
1. I recognize and accept all students with respect for their individual and shared cultural characteristics.		
2. I provide all students with information, access, and opportunities to learn more about themselves, one another, and society in the context of culture.		
3. I ensure that all learning connects with individual academic and cultural backgrounds.		
4. For professional development, I am learning more about my own cultural characteristics.		
5. For professional development, I am learning more about the cultural characteristics of the various student populations attending my school.		
NE: Negotiate and Evaluate Curriculum and Content		
1. I teach all students about other cultures in all parts of the curriculum.		
2. I support all students to achieve high standards throughout the curriculum and instruction.		
3. I provide all students with a variety of avenues of expression, alongside opportunities to exchange outcomes with peers aligned with multiple forms of assessment.		
4. For professional development, I examine various textbooks and supplementary materials to infuse more cultural connections into the curriculum.		
5. For professional development, I seek new instructional strategies that infuse more cultural connections into the instruction.		

E: Establish Community and Context		
1. I ensure that all students feel safe, welcomed, and wanted in the classroom and school.		
2. I have transformed my classroom into a learning community that is student centered and learner driven.		
3. I provide students with multiple opportunities to contribute to and participate in classroom and school functions.		
4. For professional development, I have visited a classroom that is focused on learning communities.		
5. For professional development, I have attended a workshop on learning communities.		
SE: Seek and Engage in Collaboration and Construction		
1. I teach students the processes and encourage them to construct new learning collaboratively.		
2. I group students so they learn more information about one another and society.		
3. I teach all students the processes for interacting appropriately with people like and unlike themselves.		
4. For professional development, I practice collaboration with a teammate on a project.		
5. For professional development, I read professional literature to learn more about collaborating with students.		
S: Spark Conversations and Climate		
1. I teach all students about bias, prejudice, and stereotyping.		
2. I teach all students about democratic principles, educational equity, human rights, and social justice.		
3. I give all students voice, choice, and ownership in their learning.		

4. For professional development, I have attended a workshop to become more aware of and reduce bias in the classroom.		
5. For professional development, I have visited an agency focused on human rights to learn more about the content and practices.		
SW: Strengthen and Weave Together Complexities and Controversies		
1. I teach all students the complex topics and issues related to the curriculum and instruction to increase higher-order thinking skills and applications in the world.		
2. I provide all students with authentic opportunities to engage in critical thinking, problem solving, and decision making related to the curriculum.		
3. I provide all students with multiple opportunities to participate in discussions about culturally based controversial topics and issues.		
4. For professional development, I engage in curricular mapping to connect appropriate controversial issues to the curriculum.		
5. For professional development, I meet with a mentor to discuss instructional strategies for conducting classroom meetings.		
W: Waken Compassion and Commitment		
1. I teach all students the concepts and practices of care and compassion in the context of the curriculum and the community.		
2. I provide all students with opportunities to organize and participate in meaningful service learning projects.		
3. I teach all students the concepts and practices of commitment and the benefits for future learning and living.		
4. For professional development, I have attended a seminar emphasizing compassion for a community concern.		
5. For professional development, I have read a biography of an individual who displayed compassion and commitment.		

NW: Nurture and Welcome Challenges and Changes		
1. I teach all students how challenges exist through all parts of the curriculum.		
2. I teach all students skills related to conflict management.		
3. I teach all students about the change process and engage in authentic opportunities to practice the change process.		
4. For professional development, I talk with a mentor who has experience with challenges and changes in one's professional practices.		
5. For professional development, I reflect on my personal life, have identified one challenge related to cultural competence, and practice making changes.		

Resource C

Websites

Advancement Project
http://www.advancementproject.org

Affirmative Action and Diversity Project
http://aad.english.ucsb.edu/

African American Newspaper
http://www.afro.com

American Association of Retired Persons
http://www.aarp.org/

American Civil Liberties Union
http://www.aclu.org/

American Indian Library Association
http://www.ailanet.org/

American Indian Library Association: Native American Sites
http://www.nativeculturelinks.com/indians.html

American Indian Movement
http://www.aimovement.org/

American Library Association: Banned Book List
**http://www.ala.org/ala/issuesadvocacy/banned/bannedbook
sweek/index.cfm**

Amnesty International
http://www.amnesty.org/

Anti-Defamation League
http://www.adl.org/education/

Anti-Racist and Multicultural Education
http://www.pep.educ.ubc.ca/anti.html

Association for Childhood International: Global Guidelines for Early Childhood Education and Care in the 21st Century
http://acei.org/education/guidelines/

Association of Teacher Education Standards
http://www.ate1.org/pubs/uploads/tchredstds0308.pdf

Bilingual Books for Kids
http://www.bilingualbooks.com/

Brit Kid
http://www.britkid.org

The BUENO Center
http://www.colorado.edu/education/BUENO/

Bureau of the Census
http://www.census.gov

The Center for Advancement of Learning and Teaching: Inclusive Teaching
http://depts.washington.edu/cidrweb/inclusive/

Center for Applied Linguistics (CA)
http://www.cal.org

Center for Effective Collaboration and Practice
http://cecp.air.org/cultural/

Center for Multicultural Education
http://education.washington.edu/cme/

Center for Multilingual Multicultural Research
http://www.usc.edu/dept/education/CMMR/

Center for Research on Education, Diversity & Excellence
http://www.cal.org/crede/

Center for the Prevention of Hate Violence
http://www.preventinghate.org/

Center for the Study of the White American Culture (A Multiracial Organization)
http://www.euroamerican.org/

Center for World Indigenous Studies
http://www.cwis.org/wwwvl/indig-vl.html

Children L.E.A.D. Project
http://www.childrenlead.org/

Children's Defense Fund
http://www.childrensdefense.org/

The Civil Rights Project
http://www.civilrightsproject.ucla.edu/

CoAction Connection
http://www.antiracism.com

Conflict Resolution Research Resource Institute
http://www.cri.cc/

Core Knowledge
http://www.coreknowledge.org

Cornucopia of Disability Information
http://codi.buffalo.edu/

Cultural Arts Center for Teachers and Students
http://www.carts.org/

The Densho Project
http://www.densho.org

Digital History
http://www.digitalhistory.uh.edu/

Discover Human Rights
http://www.discoverhumanrights.org/

Diversity Forum
http://www.diversityforum.com/

Diversity Web
http://www.diversityweb.org/

EdChange
http://edchange.org/index.html

EdChange Multicultural Pavilion
http://www.edchange.org/multicultural

Education Alliance at Brown University
http://www.alliance.brown.edu/

Education Development Center
http://www.edc.org

Educational Justice
http://www.edjustice.org

Educators for Social Responsibility
http://esrnational.org/

Educator's Reference Desk
**http://www.eduref.org/cgi-bin/lessons.cgi/Social_Studies/Multicultural_
Education**

Electronic Magazine of Multicultural Education
http://www.eastern.edu/publications/emme/current.html

Facing History and Ourselves
http://www.facinghistory.org

Family Diversity Projects
http://www.familydiv.org/

Family Village
http://familyvillage.wisc.edu/index.html

Forum for Education
http://www.forumforeducation.org

The Free Child Project
http://freechild.org/ReadingList/socialchange.htm

Gay, Lesbian, and Straight Education Network
http://www.glsen.org/

GIRLTECH
http://www.girltech.com

Global School Net
http://www.globalschoolnet.org/index.cfm

Global Source Education
http://www.globalsourcenetwork.org/

Greenpeace
http://www.greenpeace.org/usa/

Harvard Graduate School of Education: Websites for Educators
http://gseweb.harvard.edu/library/educator_resources.html

Hispanic America: USA
http://www.neta.com/~1stbooks/content.htm

Hispanic Online
http://www.hispaniconline.com

Holidays Around the World
http://www.gourmetgiftbaskets.com/Holidays-Around-The-World.asp

Human Rights Education Association
http://www.hrea.org

Human Rights Resource Center
http://www.hrusa.org

Information Collection
http://www.xs4all.nl/~swanson/history/chapter0102.html

Interesting Things for ESL Students
http://www.manythings.org/

International Digital Children's Library
http://en.childrenslibrary.org/

The Kennedy Center: America, A Home for Every Culture
http://artsedge.kennedy-center.org/content/2316/

Keystone College Diversity Websites
http://web.keystone.edu/Library/Subj_Pages/diversity.html#glbt

Kidlink: Multicultural Calendar
http://www.kidlink.org

Lanic
http://lanic.utexas.edu

Lee and Low Books
http://www.leeandlow.com/

Lesbian, Gay, Bisexual, Transgendered, Queer, Two Spirit, Intersex Group
http://www.ssw.washington.edu/glbtq

Leveraging Diversity
http://www.leveragingdiversity.com/

Library of Congress
http://www.loc.gov/index.html

Media Awareness Network
http://www.media-awareness.ca/english/index.cfm

Minnesota Advocates for Human Rights
http://www.mnadvocates.org

Multicultural Book Reviews
http://www.isomedia.com/homes/jmele/joe.html

Multicultural Education and Ethnic Groups: Selected Internet Sources
http://wwwlibrary.csustan.edu/lboyer/multicultural/main.htm

Multicultural Math Fair
http://mathforum.org/alejandro/mathfair/index.html

Multicultural Media
http://www.multiculturalmedia.com

National Association for Bilingual Education
http://www.nabe.org/

National Association for Ethnic Studies
http://www.ethnicstudies.org/

National Association for Multicultural Education
http://www.nameorg.org

National Center for Cultural Competence
http://www11.georgetown.edu/research/gucchd/nccc/

National Center for Curriculum Transformation Resources for Women
http://pages.towson.edu/ncctrw/

National Clearinghouse for English Language Acquisition
http://www.ncela.gwu.edu/

National Council of La Raza
http://www.nclr.org/

National Day of Silence
http://www.dayofsilence.org/index.cfm

National Immigration Forum
http://www.immigrationforum.org

National Multicultural Institute
http://www.nmci.org/

National Organization for Women
http://www.now.org/

National Organization on Disability
http://www.nod.org/

National Society for Latino Professionals
http://network.nshp.org/

National Women's History Project
http://www.nwhp.org/

Native Web
http://www.nativeweb.org

New Horizons for Learning
http://www.newhorizons.org

New Horizons for Learning: Multicultural Education
**http://www.newhorizons.org/strategies/multicultural/front_
multicultural.htm**

New York Metropolitan Martin Luther King Jr. Center for Nonviolence
http://www.nym.sunyeoc.org/home.asp

No Name-Calling Week
http://www.nonamecallingweek.org/cgi-bin/iowa/home.html

North Central Regional Educational Library: Multicultural Education
**http://www.ncrel.org/sdrs/areas/issues/educatrs/presrvce/pe3lk
1.htm**

Northern Arizona University: Multicultural Education Internet Resource Guide
http://jan.ucc.nau.edu/~jar/Multi.html

Office of Bilingual Education and Minority Language Affairs
http://www.ed.gov/about/offices/list/oela/index.html

Oyate
http://www.oyate.org

Passports: Cultural Competence for Teachers
**http://www.opb.org/education/minisites/culturalcompetence/
teachers.html**

Paths of Learning
http://www.pathsoflearning.org/resources_Useful_Sites.php

PBS

http://www.pbs.org

PBS: Africans in America

http://www.pbs.org/wgbh/aia/home.html

Peace Corps Worldwise Schools

http://www.peacecorps.gov/wws/

Pew Hispanic Center

http://pewhispanic.org/

Questia

http://www.questia.com/Index.jsp?CRID=multicultural_educa tion&OFFID=se1

Racism, No Way!

http://www.racismnoway.com.au

Responsive Classroom

http://www.responsiveclassroom.org

Rethinking Schools

http://www.rethinkingschools.org

Rutgers School of Communication and Information: Vandergrift's Children's Literature Page

http://www.scils.rutgers.edu/~kvander/ChildrenLit/index.html

Sites for Teachers

http://www.sitesforteachers.com/index25.html

Social Studies Lessons: Unite the School

http://www.coe.uh.edu/archive/sstudies/sstudies_lessons/ssles3 .htm

Social Studies School Services

http://socialstudies.com

The Southern Institute for Education and Research

http://www.southerninstitute.info/index.jsp

Southern Poverty Law Center
http://www.splcenter.org

Teacher Planet
http://www.lessonplans4teachers.com/

Teachers of English to Speakers of Other Languages
http://www.tesol.org

Teaching for Change
http://www.teachingforchange.org

Teaching Tolerance
http://www.tolerance.org

Understanding Prejudice
http://www.understandingprejudice.org

UNICEF
http://www.unicef.org/

United Nations
http://www.un.org/

United Nations Cyberschoolbus: Racism and Anti-Racist Resources and Organisations for Students and Teachers
http://www.un.org/cyberschoolbus/racism2001/orglinks.asp

United Nations Global Teaching and Learning Project: Cyberschoolbus
http://www.un.org/Pubs/CyberSchoolBus/index.shtml

University of Calgary: Diversity Toolkit
http://www.ucalgary.ca/~dtoolkit/index.htm

The University of Iowa Center for Human Rights
http://international.uiowa.edu/centers/human-rights/resources/online/organizations.asp

University of Maryland: Diversity Database
http://www.inform.umd.edu/EdRes/Topic/Diversity/

University of Maryland: Diversity Dictionary

http://www.inform.umd.edu/EdRes/Topic/Diversity/Reference/divdic.html

Urban Ed

http://www.ed.gov/pubs/ToolsforSchools/usd.html

Urban Mosaik Magazine

http://www.urbanmozaik.com/

U.S. Census Bureau: Minority Links

http://www.census.gov/newsroom/minority_links/minority_links.html

United States Department of Education

http://www.ed.gov/index.jhtml?src=a

United States Office of Civil Rights, Department of the Interior

http://www.doi.gov/diversity/

Using English.com: Resources for English as a Second Language

http://www.usingenglish.com/

WestEd

http://www.wested.org/lcd/links_bilingual.htm/

White Privilege Conference

http://www.whiteprivilegeconference.com

Women in World History

http://www.womeninworldhistory.com/index.html

Working to Improve Schools and Education: Multicultural Education and Culturally Responsive Teaching

http://www.ithaca.edu/wise/topics/multicultural.htm

Yale-New Haven Teachers Institute: Changing Attitudes in America

http://www.yale.edu/ynhti/curriculum/units/1994/4/94.04.04.x.html

References

Anderson, J. A. (1996). *Communication theory: Epistemological foundations.* New York: Guilford Press.

Asher, N. (2007). Made in the (multicultural) U.S.A.: Unpacking tensions of race, culture, gender, and sexuality in education. *Educational Researcher, 36*(2), 65–73.

Bandura, A. (1997). *Self-efficacy: The exercise of control.* New York: W. H. Freeman.

Banks, J. A. (2008). *An introduction to multicultural education* (4th ed.). Boston: Pearson.

Bergeon, B. S. (2008). Enacting a culturally responsive curriculum in a novice teacher's classroom: Encountering disequilibrium. *Urban Education, 43*(1), 4–28.

Black, P., & Wiliam, D. (1998). Assessment and classroom learning. *Assessment in Education: Principles, Policy and Practice, 5*(1), 7–73.

Christensen, L. (2000). *Reading, writing, and rising up: Teaching about social justice and the power of the written word.* Milwaukee, WI: Rethinking Schools.

Cochran-Smith, M., Davis, D., & Fries, K. (2004). Multicultural teacher education: Research, practice, and policy. In J. A. Banks & C. A. Banks (Eds.), *Handbook of research on multicultural education* (2nd ed.) (pp. 931–975). San Francisco: Jossey-Bass.

Cushner, K. (2005). *Human diversity in education: An interactive approach* (5th ed.). Boston: McGraw-Hill.

Daffen, L., & Anderson, G. L. (2009). Diversity and educational leadership: Democratic equality and the goals of schooling. In S. R. Steinberg (Ed.), *Diversity and multiculturalism: A reader* (pp. 437–448). New York: Peter Lang.

Festinger, L., Schachter, S., & Back, K. (1950). The spatial ecology of group formation. In L. Festinger, S. Schachter, & K. Back (Eds.), *Social pressure in informal groups: A study of human factors in housing* (pp. 141–161). Stanford, CA: Stanford University Press.

Freire, P. (1970). *Pedagogy of the oppressed.* New York: Continuum.

Gallavan, N. P. (2007). Seven perceptions that influence novice teachers' efficacy and cultural competence. *Praxis: The Center for Multicultural Education, 2*(1), 2–22.

Gay, G. (2000). *Culturally responsive teaching: Theory, research, & practice.* New York: Teachers College Press.

Giroux, H. A. (1988). *Schooling and the struggle for public life: Critical pedagogy in the modern age.* Minneapolis: University of Minnesota Press.

Hollins, E. R. (1996). *Culture in school learning: Revealing the deep meaning* (2nd ed.). New York: Routledge.

Huffman, S., & Rickman, W. (2004). Technology planning: The SIMPLE model. *Educational Technology, 44*(4), 36–40.

Jacobs, H. H. (1997). *Mapping the big picture: Integrating curriculum and assessment K–12.* Alexandria, VA: Association for Supervision and Curriculum Development.

Leonard, B., & Plotnikoff, G. (2000). Awareness: The heart of cultural competence. *AACN Clinical Issues: Advanced Practice in Acute & Critical Care, 11*(1), 51–59.

Lortie, D. C. (1975). *Schoolteacher: A sociological study.* Chicago: University of Chicago Press.

McCann, T. M., & Johannessen, L. (2008). Retaining quality teachers is the real test. *English Journal, 98*(2), 86–88.

McIntosh, P. (1989, July/Aug). White privilege: Unpacking the invisible knapsack. *Peace and Freedom,* 10–12.

Merton, R. K. (1936). The unanticipated consequences of purposive social action. *American Sociological Review, 1*(6), 894–904.

Oakes, J., & Lipton, M. (1999). *Teaching to change the world.* Boston: McGraw-Hill.

Oakley, A. (1997). Human agents and rationality in Max Weber's social economics. *International Journal of Social Economics, 24*(7–9), 812–830.

Ogbu, J. U. (2000). Adaptation to minority status and impact on school success. *Theory into Practice, 31*(4), 287–295.

Oliva, P. (2004). *Developing the curriculum* (4th ed.). New York: Longman.

Pohan, C. A., & Aguilar, T. E. (2001). Measuring educators' beliefs about diversity in personal and professional contexts. *American Educational Research Journal, 38*(1), 159–182.

Reeves, D. (2009). *Leading change in your school: How to conquer myths, build commitment, and get results.* Alexandria, VA: Association for Supervision and Curriculum Development.

Resnick, L. (1987). *Education and learning to think.* Washington, DC: National Academy Press.

Schommer, M. (1990). Effects of beliefs about the nature of knowledge on comprehension. *Journal of Educational Psychology, 82,* 498–504.

Sleeter, C. (2009). Developing teacher epistemological sophistication about multicultural curriculum: A case study. *Action in Teacher Education, 31*(1), 3–13.

Sleeter, C., & McLaren, P. (2009). Origins of multiculturalism. In W. Au (Ed.), *Rethinking multicultural education: Teaching for racial and cultural justice* (pp. 17–20). Milwaukee, WI: Rethinking Schools.

Thye, S. R. (2000). A status value theory of power in exchange networks. *American Sociological Review, 65*(3), 407–432.

Van Manen, M. (1997). *Researching lived experience: Human science for an action sensitive pedagogy.* London: Althouse Press.

Vygotsky, L. (1978). *Mind in society.* London: Harvard University Press.

Ward, M. J., & Ward, C. J. (2003). Promoting cross-cultural competence in preservice teachers through second language use. *Education, 123,* 532–536.

Wiggins, G., & McTighe, J. (2005). *Understanding by design* (2nd ed.). Upper Saddle River, NJ: Prentice Hall.

Index

CORWIN
A SAGE Company

The Corwin logo—a raven striding across an open book—represents the union of courage and learning. Corwin is committed to improving education for all learners by publishing books and other professional development resources for those serving the field of PreK–12 education. By providing practical, hands-on materials, Corwin continues to carry out the promise of its motto: **"Helping Educators Do Their Work Better."**